CREATING THE FUTURE

The Massachusetts Comeback
and Its Promise for America

Michael S. Dukakis and Rosabeth Moss Kanter

SUMMIT BOOKS
New York · London · Toronto · Sydney · Tokyo

SUMMIT BOOKS
SIMON & SCHUSTER BUILDING
ROCKEFELLER CENTER
1230 AVENUE OF THE AMERICAS
NEW YORK, NEW YORK 10020

PUBLISHED BY SUMMIT BOOKS

SUMMIT BOOKS AND COLOPHON ARE TRADEMARKS
OF SIMON & SCHUSTER INC.

DESIGNED BY LEVAVI & LEVAVI
MANUFACTURED IN THE UNITED STATES OF AMERICA

10   9   8   7   6   5   4   3   2   1

LIBRARY OF CONGRESS CATALOGING IN PUBLICATION DATA

ISBN 0-671-65882-4

Contents

This book is dedicated to the true architects
of the Massachusetts Comeback—the
hardworking, innovative, talented men and
women who live, work, and invest in
Massachusetts.

Preface and Acknowledgments

This is an unusual and perhaps unprecedented collaboration, combining the record and perspective of a sitting governor with the case studies and analysis of a business expert. We each brought unique contributions, and we each have an outstanding staff to thank for their invaluable assistance.

Michael Dukakis was responsible for identifying the issues, defining the underlying philosophies and policy recommendations, and recounting the history of the Commonwealth's programs and policies. The Dukakis portions of this book benefited greatly from the numerous policy and editorial contributions of Alden S. Raine and John DeVillars. Mr. Raine is Director of the Governor's Office of Economic Development; Mr. DeVillars is the Governor's Chief of Operations. Both authors extend their appreciation for the help and support they provided in the development of this book.

Rosabeth Kanter was responsible for field research resulting in case studies of businesses, cities, and people affected by state programs; providing the intellectual data-based framework for innovation and contributing to policy recommendations; and organizing and conceptualizing the material. Especially valuable contributions to the Kanter portions were made by Paul Myers, Cynthia Ingols, and Barry Stein, who were involved in every phase, from interviewing to analysis. Other important members of her research team included Elisabeth Richardson, Peter Raymond, Hugh O'Brien, James Phills, Alistair Williamson, Andrea Larson, and Kathleen Chaudhry. Support for field research on thirty Massachusetts companies (part of an ongoing study of entrepreneurship and innovation) was provided by the Division of Research at the Harvard Business School, whose help is gratefully acknowledged.

Even though this is a collaboration, it is also an attempt to define an approach to government from the perspective of a government leader. Therefore, we have decided to take the unusual step of telling most of the story as Michael Dukakis saw it. Rosabeth Kanter's business case studies are set apart in the text, and she offers her own views and research summary in the Introduction.

CREATING
THE FUTURE

Investment Economics and the Politics of Partnership: Lessons from the Massachusetts Experience

by Rosabeth Moss Kanter

There has been increasing debate recently on the proper role of government in fostering economic health. State governments have been overlooked in the discussion. It's not simply a matter of what a state government *should* do (although that question has certainly been alive and well); it's what state government *can* do as a matter of practical reality.

There has been a growing assumption that the role of any government but the federal government has been eclipsed and rendered less relevant by powerful technologies, a global economy, and the huge, overarching federal apparatus itself.

The idea of Massachusetts—or any state—somehow transcending these enormous macroeconomic forces conveys a quaintly romantic quality, akin to Cambridge and Palo Alto at one time declaring themselves "nuclear-free zones," as if that might somehow disarm (pun intended) the superpowers. After all, states do not set monetary policy or trade rules, two of the hottest items in the competitiveness debate.

All the more reason, then, to look at Massachusetts' recent economic success. It was not too long ago that the state was mockingly referred to as Taxachusetts and the "antibusiness" state. But since the mid-1970s, the turnaround has been stunning —from the tattered remnants of the early industrial economy to the Mecca of the Information Age in less than fifteen years. By 1987, Massachusetts had the lowest unemployment rate of any industrial state and was the only state to receive high marks in every category in a *Business Week* review of states' support for business. Massachusetts programs were being emulated in many other states, and Governor Michael Dukakis was voted America's number one governor by his peers.

Massachusetts performed its economic miracle in an environment characterized simultaneously by declining real wealth, increased foreign competition, and growing doubt about governmental action, expressed through voter-induced limitation on state and local taxes.

Thus, the Massachusetts experience of the past decade, with its rather remarkable comeback from assumed economic oblivion, is worth careful attention, and not simply because Governor Dukakis, the present CEO, is a candidate for "promotion" (he's running for president). Clearly, there is something for America to learn from the so-called Massachusetts miracle.

To see just what the lessons are, I spent nearly two years examining the state's support for business innovation.

I first focused on this issue in the fall of 1985, when I joined Governor Dukakis and others on a tour of innovative companies in the state, companies responsible for developing new technologies and creating jobs. This effort led to my membership on the Governor's Advisory Council on Innovation. As chair of the council's Business Enhancement Subcommittee in 1986, I listened to scores of business, labor, and community leaders describe their experiences with the state, and I reviewed piles of documents on state programs and policies. I became interested enough in the role of the local environment in innovation and entrepreneurship to put that topic on my academic research agenda. Starting in September 1986, my Harvard Business School research group examined first hand and in depth thirty innovating firms throughout Massachusetts—new and old, high tech and no tech, large and small, independent and subsidiaries of corporate giants. We visitited artificial intelligence gurus and cranberry packagers, biomedical engineers and egg producers, as well as training sites and state program offices. We interviewed numerous business leaders.

We concluded, like many, that macroeconomic forces, such as demand for the products produced by Massachusetts-based companies, underlay most of the boom. But we also discovered that the state government's actions, under Dukakis's leadership, had found ways to augment and leverage the private initiative of innovators and entrepreneurs, creating an "economic echo" effect.

There are forces at work upon any economy which can be far more powerful than the government. A government can work only to shape the impact of these forces.

Some of the raw materials for the boom in Massachusetts were assembled long before Michael Dukakis became governor. Route 128, the perimeter road around Boston, had long been regarded as "America's Technology Highway." The seeds for the shift to high technology had been sown by advanced research during World War II, and the Massachusetts Institute of Technology research laboratories alone spawned as many as 150 companies, some funded by the venture capital firms clustered in the area. One of the most spectacular successes was American research and development's investment in Digital Equipment Corporation, founded in 1957 and, thirty years later, a $7 billion company employing almost 110,000 people worldwide—about 30,000 in Massachusetts alone. Harvard University, which celebrated its 350th anniversary in 1986, is another Massachusetts institution adding to the state's reputation as a center for brainpower.

So when the world economy moved into the Information Age, demanding high tech and brainpower, Massachusetts was ready.

And when Dukakis took office for the first time in 1975, he was ready to accelerate the transformation as well as to aid those individuals and firms who would be dislocated by such economic shifts. The state's economic development policies were thus added to the other forces acting on the Massachusetts economy.

But clearly, state government was just one force among many. Ronald Ferguson and Helen Ladd of Harvard's Kennedy School of Government conducted a review of the impact of economic development policy in Massachusetts, as part of a four-state comparison sponsored by the Committee for Economic Development. They argued that:

> The short-term impacts of state economic policy can be positive on the firms and geographic areas directly affected. And with time, these effects may diffuse through the state's economy and accumulate. But state-sponsored economic initiatives are neither quick fixes for weak economies nor certified elixirs for healthy ones (Ronald F. Ferguson and Helen F. Ladd, "Economic Performance and Economic Development Policy in Massachusetts" [Discussion paper D86–2, JFK School of Government, Harvard University, The State, Local, and Intergovernmental Center, May 1986]).

But while cautious about giving state government credit for causing the remarkable turnaround, Ferguson and Ladd do conclude that state initiatives did two important things: they helped to attract growth to some depressed central cities and slow-growing regions, and they also helped to sustain the state's revival once it began. If state government actions did not *cause* the boom, they did help *deepen* and *broaden* it.

This "economic echo" reverberated throughout numerous industries besides high tech, throughout parts of the state besides the Route 128 technology cluster, and throughout groups of people besides highly skilled professionals. Normally, a boom in one place can mean bust in another, even within the borders of a single state. Arguably, there would have been no *Massachusetts* comeback if Dukakis had not worked hard to spread the process of economic growth evenly.

And while the boom was still felt, the state had already begun

to lay the foundation for future growth by improving the infrastructure and supporting new technologies that could fuel con-
tinuing booms.

Dukakis was able to do this by wise use of the tools that already
existed—taking further advantage of "natural" advantages—and
by imaginative creation of new ones. His administration tapped
federal funds—using Urban Development Action Grants (UDAG)
and Job Training Partnership Act funds, for example, more vig-
orously and extensively than many other states. Ordinary government spending for such items as roads was used to help
introduce new commerce into depressed areas. The existing state
university system was revamped and strengthened. At the same
time, Dukakis stressed innovation—resulting in such creative
new programs as ET Choices, a pioneering employment-and-
training program that moved people from welfare to work; and
the Massachusetts Technology Development Corporation, the
first state-run venture capital firm in the nation.

Just what is there for a country to learn from the events in
Massachusetts?

To say that Massachusetts can be held up as a model for the
nation is simplistic. Because the experience of any one state is
always just a single case, unique in some ways, and because we
cannot easily extrapolate from a single state to the nation, we
should be wary of misplaced concreteness—the item-by-item assessment of whether what worked in Massachusetts would work
elsewhere. The real lessons of this story are *not* about whether
Program X would work equally well in the Farm Belt or whether
Program Y, appropriate at the state level, could translate to the
federal level.

Instead, this is really a story about leadership. It shows us how
a leader can use the economic development tools at hand—in
this case, the ones available at the state level—to begin to realize
a vision that a healthy economy can bring opportunity for all.

As Ferguson and Ladd put it:

The process through which government officials worked with representatives in shaping economic policy clearly affected the state's

political culture and business climate. People from government, labor, business, academic, and other backgrounds improved their ability to work together cooperatively and this, among other things, enhanced the state's capacity to effectively conduct its political and economic affairs. This suggests that the method by which Massachusetts formulated economic policy over the past decade is probably as important as the programmatic details of the new initiatives (Ferguson and Ladd, "Economic Performance").

Michael Dukakis had an economic vision. He developed a clear and comprehensive strategy for acting on the vision. And he operated as a chief executive in ways that maximized the success of the strategy.

The *vision* rested on an understanding that entrepreneurship and innovation provided the basis for growth in an advanced industrial economy.

The *strategy* defined the role of government as investing and encouraging private initiative, rather than taxing and spending.

The *operating mode* was one of hands-on leadership, coalition building, and the forging of partnerships.

In short, in the Massachusetts story we can see in action the marriage of two emerging American ideals: *investment economics* coupled with the *politics of partnership*.

It was Michael Dukakis's mission to support a healthy economy that would provide opportunity for all citizens. This chance to participate in the economic mainstream would be a result of innovation and entrepreneurship—the new businesses and the improvements to existing businesses that could create jobs.

His vision rested on a belief that public investment could encourage and support private initiative, especially in stimulating economic growth for depressed neighborhoods and the disadvantaged. It was therefore very different from the two major alternatives then in vogue: the free market fantasies of so-called trickledown economics, in which the government's role was to stay out of the way of business; or the redistributive view that government had to take from the currently prosperous "haves" in order to provide for the "have nots." Instead, it was a vision of government-as-public-investor leveraging the talents of enterprising citizens.

In Dukakis's view, the entrepreneurial spirit occupied center stage.

His emphasis on innovation and entrepreneurship squares well with the data about sources of economic growth, particularly in today's competitive global economy. As I discovered in researching my 1983 book, *The Change Masters* (New York: Simon & Schuster), where America was still ahead in world markets, it led because of innovation. In certain vital, innovative industries such as computers, pharmaceuticals, medical electronics, and telecommunications, the United States was ahead even of Japan, and though Japan was the world's number two exporter of large computers, a sizable share of those were made by IBM of Japan. When American companies began to slip, even in these industries, it was because of a failure to invest in creating new technologies or innovating manufacturing processes.

Technological innovation provides an economic advantage, and entrepreneurship helps translate this into jobs. Throughout the United States, new jobs tend to come from innovation-related growth spurts in existing enterprises and from the development of new enterprises.

David Birch's data base covering 5.6 million firms—82 percent of all private sector employment—makes the case that all areas of the United States lose jobs at the same rate. So regions are differentiated, then, by their ability to create jobs, which in turn is a function of high rates of innovation. Furthermore, job-creating firms tend to be small and new. Two-thirds of all jobs created between 1969 and 1976 were created by firms with twenty or fewer employees, and 80 percent were created by firms with a hundred or fewer. And 80 percent of new jobs came from firms four years old or younger. (David L. Birch, *Choosing a Place to Grow: Business Location Decisions in the 1970's* [Cambridge, Mass.: MIT Program on Neighborhood and Regional Change, 1981].)

Dukakis's emphasis on innovation and entrepreneurship certainly recognized the importance of new ventures and smaller businesses. But he also included innovation in large, established businesses. Revitalizing mature industries and ensuring economic diversity were important parts of the vision, as a state Commission on the Future of Mature Industries urged. After all, past problems in Massachusetts (like current problems in Texas and other states that are suffering) came from overspecialization, overdependence on one or two key industries. Furthermore, large firms still accounted for the bulk of established employment, and the fate of many small firms was tied directly to the fortunes of their large-firm customers. Finally, to seek the new without helping improve and save the old would place an undue burden on people who would be dislocated by abrupt economic shifts. Renewing traditional industries was thus as necessary as encouraging the development of new ones.

The goal of this probusiness stance was clear: to create jobs and to ensure opportunity for all people. Therefore, it was important to channel the state's investments in ways that would indeed bring these jobs to the people and places that needed them.

Dukakis's strategy for achieving his economic goals derived from a central premise about the role of government: Government is not here to tax and spend but, rather, to invest. Government should invest in ways that leverage private investment and private initiative. Its role is not to substitute for private sector activity but to augment it—filling gaps and providing an extra boost for efforts that serve a public purpose.

I have identified five key components of the strategy.

1. *Support the development and use of new technologies in ventures that will create jobs.* This is a long-winded way of saying: support entrepreneurs. But Governor Dukakis was not just talking about entrepreneurs involved in starting new businesses. He also wanted to help finance new product development and technical retooling in established firms.

The Dukakis strategy placed particular emphasis on making sure that the people with innovative ideas could get their businesses started or retooled. Massachusetts has long been a center for venture capital, but it is still possible for good ideas to fall through the cracks. What the state has done is to fill in the holes through which many firms might otherwise fall. Mechanisms such as the Massachusetts Technology Development Corporation and the Massachusetts Product Development Corporation, both quasi-public agencies, were developed to counter market short-falls in the recognition that there are fads and fancies in venture capital that may not adequately reflect economic potential.

New ventures are the most dependent on already-existing sources of capital, of human resources, and of technical expertise in their local area. Unlike large, established firms, they are in no position to move anywhere or supply most of their needs inter-nally or even, in many cases, to pick up and move to any location in any area. In this sense, all entrepreneurship is inherently local. New companies are usually started where the founders already are. Thus, the more easily they can find what they need to get started right where they are, the greater the likelihood of success, because they can then concentrate more directly on building and running the business. So it is helpful for the state to make avail-able locally the tools entrepreneurs need—through financing mechanisms, educational programs, and even technical assis-tance.

2. *Concentrate resources to create critical mass effects.* Instead of trying to make everything happen everywhere, the Dukakis administration built on the existing strengths and specialties of an area. The Massachusetts Centers of Excellence Program, for example, bundled a number of existing education and research efforts under a common label in order to concentrate research-and-development resources on the indigenous strengths of a re-gion—plastics in Western Massachusetts, marine technologies along the coast, and so forth. This would create a critical mass in each area that could, it was hoped, attract brainpower to the area and lead to the formation of many more new ventures than if left to chance.

It is not accidental that this idea is widely credited to an economist, Evelyn Murphy, who was Dukakis's secretary of economic affairs before becoming lieutenant governor in his third administration. There is ample evidence supporting the proposition that a critical mass of firms and people sharing particular technical specialties creates helpful "agglomeration effects," as economists put it. For example, a higher density in an area of firms employing new technologies appears to be associated with higher financial performance of those firms, according to a study comparing the returns of California's Silicon Valley and Route 128 companies against their more scattered counterparts nationwide (Joanne Hill and Joel L. Naroff, "The Effect of Location on the Performance of High Technology Firms," *Financial Management* [Spring 1984], 27–36). People with the right skills are attracted to the area, firms formally and informally trade knowledge and personnel, support services grow up to meet the industry's special needs, there are local markets for components manufacturers, and parts of current companies are spun off to create new ones.

Many of the studies of the electronics and computer boom in Massachusetts could be retitled "In Praise of MIT." The private universities, and in particular the Massachusetts Institute of Technology, have been perhaps the most important single factor, if we have to pick one. Edward Roberts of MIT's Sloan School of Management has shown that of 216 high-tech companies in Boston, 156 (72 percent) were created in MIT labs or departments (Marshall J. Goldman, "Building a Mecca for High Technology," *Technology Review* 87 [May-June, 1984]: 6–8). Becoming aware of this fact, Dukakis began to focus on improving the public university system enough to create similar masses of technical talent throughout the state. Early in 1987, Massachusetts announced a $1 billion capital improvement plan for public colleges, with nearly a third going to strengthen the University of Lowell. The University of Lowell was an outgrowth of the state-backed revitalization of the city of Lowell, and it already ranks fifth in the United States as a source of technical employees for the Massachusetts high-tech industry.

3: *Focus investment on neglected areas and people.* Helping the disadvantaged was one area where Dukakis's solutions were particularly innovative, making investment economics the centerpiece of a political philosophy that could take the place of old-fashioned welfare economics. Instead of taxing the rich to send welfare checks to the poor, Dukakis found ways to encourage the sources of jobs to go directly to the people who needed them.

There were two principal means for accomplishing this. One brought the people to the jobs, the second brought the jobs to the people. Both were clearly important pieces of the strategy, for experience teaches us that attempts to do one without the other —training without jobs or new industry without a skilled workforce—ultimately fail.

The first mechanism involved a heavy emphasis on skills training for the disadvantaged. The Commonwealth Employment Forum, supported by a foundation grant, went abroad to seek alternatives for skills training, then recommended overall approaches to integrate the work of nearly twenty state agencies involved in training. Programs were designed and carried out specifically to help people whose shortfalls were not of their own making: those thrown out of work by economic sea changes and closed enterprises, with energy but no longer marketable skills; those with a willingness to learn but no resources, often with dependents and forced to rely on welfare; and those with no relevant work experience, or with language problems, but with a will and a wish to work. ET Choices, an expanded Bay State Skills Corporation (begun under a predecessor), and various industrial partnerships all made a critical contribution.

The second mechanism was the identification of areas with higher-than-average unemployment as "Targets for Opportunity." Targeting state investment on those geographic areas, coupled with attractive packages of incentives for new businesses to locate there, helped speed up the job-creation process and concentrate it where the initial spark could find the fuel to catch fire and a little protection from economic winds. Apart from purely

formal programs, this also reflected a deliberate tilt in state responsiveness, right across the agency roster. Possible investments in urban centers got priority attention. And every unit of
the Commonwealth encouraged and supported action in targeted
areas.

4. *Make it easy for established firms to do business.* The Dukakis strategy, particularly starting in his second administration,
emphasized that intangible factor called "business climate." In
his first term, he had concentrated on fiscal stability, balancing
the budget, and he had not always pleased the business community. He lost to a more conservative competitor in 1978. Upon his
reelection in 1982, the strategy became more direct: make Massachusetts an attractive place to conduct business. This took two
forms: (1) state investment in numerous infrastructure improvements, including transportation, housing, and an attractive environment, especially those that would attract business—and thus,
jobs—to targeted regions; and (2) a helpful, facilitative attitude
on the part of state officials, ensuring less red tape and the support of vital industries with marketing efforts.

The voluminous literature on site selection by established
businesses is clear on a few points that support Dukakis's investments in infrastructure. To attract business—and therefore jobs
—to an area requires a high-quality infrastructure, the presence
of a technically skilled work force, outstanding educational institutions, and a high quality of life (Bruce N. Wardrep, "Factors
Which Play Major Roles in Location Decision," *Industrial Development*" 153 [July-August, 1985]: 72–76). These are generally
much more important, studies show, than low wage rates. And
contrary to popular belief, tax rates do not play much of a role in
location decision. Low taxes may be a tiebreaker between otherwise similar areas, but they may also be a negative factor in some
cases if they indicate poor public amenities (Roger W. Schmenner, "Look Beyond the Obvious in Plant Location," *Harvard
Business Review* 57 [January-February, 1979]: 126–32). Still, Dukakis added fiscal stability to infrastructure improvements as a
way to attract and keep businesses in the state.

Cutting government red tape was a second important agenda.

State agencies under Dukakis tried to operate as if they were just another private source of assistance. The differences between state and private support were minimized, and difficulties or preliminaries typically associated with government assistance were muted. Dukakis himself intervened to speed up the process of getting public funds for economic development, as in the financing of business relocations to Southeastern Massachusetts, an area he targeted for renewal. With respect to economic programs, the state aimed to be, in a word, nonbureaucratic.

The state also aimed to please the business community (and the citizenry) by delivering public service in an efficient, cost-effective manner. The business leaders we interviewed cited such examples as Dukakis's appointment of Ira Jackson, a well-regarded professional, to head the Department of Revenue. The department tightened enforcement and collected back taxes through an amnesty program, bringing millions of dollars into the state's budget with no new taxes.

In addition, the state began to play a proactive role in supporting certain vital industries with marketing efforts. For farmers, the label "Massachusetts Grown—and Fresher" gave a boost to local agricultural products. For software firms, a campaign to market software the same way Florida sells oranges was directed particularly at helping smaller firms. The Suppliers and Manufacturers Matching Service acted as a liaison between in-state companies for the purchase of materials and components. And the Centers of Excellence generated marketing leads for companies in their industries. All of these efforts were designed to boost business—and to make the state an attractive place for it.

5. *Secure the future by anticipating the problems of growth and solving them now.* It is plainly essential to make things happen now, to respond to immediate needs, as Governor Dukakis and his administration did. But they also recognized that, by itself, action based on present realities and needs shortchanges the future. Here is a classic political trade-off; after all, how many votes does the next generation have? Still, Dukakis emphasized the future, especially around technology, education and infrastructure.

Future economic stability is built on a foundation of technology. But what happens when today's technology is superseded by tomorrow's? The Commonwealth has therefore built a pipeline for new technology. Massachusetts developed its own R & D strategy, involving catalytic and focused investments in areas of emerging technology, such as photovoltaics and marine sciences. But technology depends critically on people—brainpower—both in its creation and its application. This naturally led to a major emphasis on long-term support for public education. And even while today's infrastructure was being rebuilt, there was an emphasis on anticipating the needs of future decades—programs for reducing future traffic congestion—a new harbor tunnel to Boston's Logan Airport and improved mass transit; for increasing future housing that people can afford; for repairing aging bridges and roads; and for protecting the environment.

Overall, the Dukakis administrations clearly innovated in a number of realms by originating creative new programs. But in many other cases, Massachusetts was not alone in its programs and policies. Some pieces of the strategy involved federal initiatives available to all the states, some were inherited from Dukakis's predecessors, and some were borrowed from other states. What was unique and noteworthy, then, was not the individual pieces but the *whole*. What was significant was that *there was a strategy*.

At a time when strategic planning has become an essential element of the operation of successful corporations, it is nice to know that government can also behave strategically. Seeing the opportunities that federal programs and state tools represented, Dukakis put them together in a coherent way, focusing them on issues and areas where it was possible to make a difference.

The Massachusetts story, finally, provides a view of how leaders can make government work. Ultimately, what is most readily transferable from the Massachusetts experience are lessons about leadership.

Effective leaders always seem to combine inspiration with pragmatism, to combine the force of their own individual personalities with the inclusion of others as collaborators and partners. In my own studies of successful innovators for *The Change Masters,* there was also a hands-on component. Leaders not only shaped and communicated a compelling vision and created coalitions and teams to implement it, but they also stayed personally involved throughout the process of change. After all, a vision— no matter how exciting—is just rhetoric until implemented. Charisma alone, without a pragmatic action orientation, is a hollow shell.

Four important leadership themes appear in Dukakis's actions in Massachusetts.

Hands-on Leadership: Spreading the Vision through Personal Presence

In a number of ways, Michael Dukakis gave meaning and importance to his economic vision through his personal involvement. He was willing to invest his own time and energy in actions that would further the vision. This investment of self, in turn, inspired others. Furthermore, his demonstrated faith in the vision gave courage to followers and helped convert skeptics.

For one thing, Dukakis made himself personally available to business and community leaders as a "tour guide" through his policy initiatives. For example, he and his top economic officials personally showcased to business executives those regions identified as Targets for Opportunity, taking them on several tours of those areas. On one such trip, he took forty leaders of industry and real-estate development through several Southeastern Massachusetts communities—an effort that ultimately led to a decision by AT&T to locate a facility there, bringing much-needed jobs to the area.

Second, Dukakis responded quickly and directly to requests for assistance. This showed up clearly in 1984 when the CEO of a company seeking to relocate in racially troubled Lawrence met with the governor to request about $7 million in assistance, including low-cost financing and public funds for infrastructure improvements and worker training. As the *National Journal* reported, it took Dukakis the "grand total of a microsecond" to instruct his staff to "Do it" (Neal R. Pierce and Carol Steinbach, "Massachusetts, After Going from Rags to Riches, Looks to Spread the Wealth," *National Journal* [May 25, 1985]: 1227–31). Within a month, the state had put together a financing package combining federal dollars with its own resources.

Third, he was readily accessible to those groups involved in local action. One of the important early state economic development priorities involved the revitalization of the old mill town of Lowell. In the beginning, it was the faith of leaders such as former Senator Paul Tsongas, the major champion of Lowell, and Dukakis himself that kept the effort afloat in light of initial skepticism—a common problem at the beginning of every innovation. George Duncan, chairman and CEO of the First Bank of Lowell, recalled in an interview the importance of the governor's personal support: "I found Dukakis and his people open-minded, ready to help us to bring people together, and they listened. . . . His support gave me the courage to continue."

Fourth, Dukakis emphasized getting things done. *Results* were more important than rhetoric. Sometimes this meant little more than doing the basic things well. The apparent simplicity of some of his programs can make it tempting to discount the leadership involved, but that would be a mistake. Early in 1986, when Dukakis started attracting national attention for the Massachusetts success story, the *Boston Globe* featured Dukakis's "lessons for the nation" in a satiric editorial page cartoon. There he was, in caricature, saying, "If you want to get people off welfare, find them jobs. If you want to raise government revenues, collect taxes." The cartoon's message was clear: the much-vaunted Massachusetts economic programs were based on simple and obvious ideas. But of course, sometimes the so-called obvious and simple solutions are the best ones.

Building Collaboration: Teams, Coalitions, and Partnerships

No leader can implement anything alone; he or she requires the active involvement of many others working together effectively. Dukakis, in particular, formed a staggering number of boards, councils, task forces, and partnerships that drew citizens from every sector into the governing process. Veteran political writer David Broder coined a term for Dukakis's leadership style, "The New Deal-Making," to describe his skill at inducing groups to put aside self-interest in the pursuit of a larger goal. This style did not work for every issue—proposals for universal health insurance and a bank to fund infrastructure improvements come to mind—but proved very effective for local economic revitalization.

Teamwork began within the state government itself. As a new governor, Dukakis inherited a bureaucracy not unlike that in other states and in Washington. Responsibility for bits and pieces of his economic development agenda were parceled out to a variety of agencies. If fragmentation were not enough to threaten the vision, then the turf protection of bureaucrats could be counted on to undermine change.

But Dukakis acted quickly to create the kind of "integrative organization" characteristic of every "change master" corporation adept at innovation (Kanter, *The Change Masters*). Step one was to get the right people. Early in his first administration, he brought together the heads of diverse agencies controlling a piece of the economic development action and named them his Development Cabinet. They were led to develop a shared vision in order to act with unity and coherence, cooperatively rather than competitively. I doubt that the state could have acted effectively at all without this teamwork at the top.

There were many other policies that were implemented effectively only because of teamwork across agencies—a dramatic change from the turf-minded bureaucracies usually found in state governments. One of the most significant was the ET (Employment and Training) Choices program that helped move welfare recipients into well-paid jobs.

Dukakis extended the coalition-crafting role outside of government to encompass the private sector as well. Through personal urging, he got a diverse set of people to work together, to blend private initiative with public resources. For example, he brought business, labor, and community leaders together in Southeastern Massachusetts in a commission charged with recommending ways to bring high technology into the area. He asked over fifty leaders in Western Massachusetts to join the new president of North Adams State College on a task force to create a new economic agenda for that troubled part of the state. His Community Development Coordinating Council is working with Boston City Hall and literally every development agency in state government to plan a new era of public and private investment in Boston's heavily minority neighborhoods of Roxbury and North Dorchester.

In some cases this meant urging people who had never met face-to-face to work effectively together. It meant encouraging groups with natural antagonisms (business and labor, town and gown, or cities that had long-standing rivalries) to suspend their differences, creating a spirit of collaboration that lasted well beyond the life of the particular board or commission. John DeRosa, cochairman of the North Berkshire economic development task force, told reporters that "It helped to have the state as the catalyst to get us together. Now we have a reason to coalesce because there's sombody to work with" (Pierce and Steinbach, "Massachusetts").

Alden Raine, head of the Governor's Office of Economic Development, also recalled:

In each area, we had to overcome real turf competition and antagonism—Thanksgiving Day high school football hatreds between towns. Getting them to cooperate—mayors and business people from the various towns to meet, to confer with us, to defer to each

other on industrial locations—was often a real pain (Pierce and
Steinbach, "Massachusetts").

In addition to creating coalitions to solve particular problems,
Dukakis also emphasized public-private partnerships, in which
state and private resources combined to address public needs.
Some he and his team developed, some he inherited but expanded in importance. The Centers of Excellence represented
one kind of partnership building close working relationships
between research educational institutions and industry. Partnerships also took the form of new "quasi-public" organizations
such as the Massachusetts Technology Development Corporation
(venture capital) or the Bay State Skills Corporation (training),
governed by joint public and private boards and only partially
funded by the state. These quasi-public organizations helped
take the "politics" out of administering key programs.

In short, Dukakis made change possible by building the alliances necessary to support it. And he mobilized literally thousands of citizens for participation in shaping their own future.
My interviews with business leaders are unequivocal on this
point, as some representative quotes indicate: As Joan Bok, chairman of New England Electric, said:

> There are so many areas where he has asked the business commu-
> nity for our contributions. No one can say they have not been
> asked! He holds meetings by topics and encourages everyone to
> talk. He brings about a dialogue, a real exchange of thoughts.

Carol Goldberg, president of Stop and Shop Companies, added:

> Dukakis is viewed as governor of all people, not just special inter-
> est groups, and he has established a positive tone by bringing to-
> gether various components of the Massachusetts economy. Public
> policy issues are tackled through coalition building, which gives a
> solid foundation to decision making.

And Joe Henson, CEO of Prime Computer, echoed these comments:

> He is committed to consensus building. He listens and hears all sides and elements in an argument. Once he has heard all opinions, he does what is best for the whole community—which is exactly what he should do. I don't always agree with everything that he does, but I do know that he has heard the arguments from business people. But he also does not pander to business people. Good government is not just focusing on what is good for business. Specifically, he has the executive, managerial, and political skills to get consensus from our broad, diverse community.

Flexibility: The Capacity to Grow and Learn

In times of rapid change, today's programs or policies can be rendered obsolete by a sudden turn of events or a challenge— economic or military—from another country. Rigid ideologies are a barrier to the mastery of change; they prevent the new ideas, the innovations, that keep the nation and its industries continually growing and adapting. Thus, leaders need to be able to grow and adapt, too.

Michael Dukakis had an enforced growth opportunity that must have seemed painful at the time. After four years as governor, he was defeated in 1978 and out of office until reelected in 1982. In retrospect, though, those four years provided a time for reflection, self-assessment, and learning. In the eyes of a wide range of observers—from his close supporters to political foes and the press—he emerged from this "moratorium" stronger, more mature, and more impressive.

The great psychoanalyst Erik Erikson first drew our attention to the role of such moratoriums in strengthening great world leaders in his work *Gandhi's Truth* (New York: Norton, 1969). Erikson was writing about Mahatma Gandhi, but the pattern recurs throughout the biographies of the truly great. After a rise to a position of prominence in which their performance is good but not extraordinary, they hit an obstacle, a defeat, that forces them into seclusion for a number of years. This period of self-examination is simultaneously humbling and focusing—a much-magnified midlife crisis. Youthful arrogance is replaced by wisdom and by commitment to a set of values that define the leader's agenda for the next phase of life.

Gandhi I, for example—premoratorium—was a lawyer in South Africa involved in securing rights for the "colored" population. Prominent but not particularly distinguished. Gandhi II—postmoratorium—returned to India with a burning passion (India's independence) and with new and highly effective methods (e.g., non violence).

The analogy is suggestive rather than exact, of course. Dukakis is not Gandhi, and there are many threads that connect Dukakis I—his first administration—to Dukakis II—the later ones. But John Cullinane, founder of Cullinet, one of the world's largest software companies, thinks the moratorium in between was indeed a major period of growth. He commented in an inverview: "I think that the four years which Dukakis spent out of office were watershed years for him. They apparently helped him to think about issues in a different way." Similarly, Dawn-Marie Driscoll, vice president and general counsel of Filene's, the well-known department store, points to a difference in style in Dukakis I and Dukakis II. In her view, Dukakis grew greatly as a leader. He became more open, more willing to listen, and less ideological—skills that dramatically increased his effectiveness with the business community. And he surrounded himself with people with these abilities.

Integrity

Perhaps the most important leadership theme has less to do with getting things done than with the personal character of the leader. What people follow, ultimately, is not a package of policies or a bundle of programs but a person. They trust that the leader is "doing the right thing," acting with integrity—or they refuse to cooperate.

For many people whom we interviewed, Michael Dukakis made them once again proud of government. Even when they disagreed with him (a frequent occurrence, especially in his first term), they trusted him to tell the truth, to act on the basis of higher principles rather than selfish or devious motivations, and to be fair. This was an important source of his success in crafting coalitions and developing partnerships. People were willing to get involved because they trusted him. Cullinet's John Cullinane put it this way:

> The number one reason I support Dukakis is because of his integrity. He also has the capacity to attract outstanding people. Issues like the economy can change, but integrity will not. That's why I place it first.

Leadership lessons may be intriguing, but many people want a more basic and hard-nosed assessment—a bottom line judgment about how much credit state government can take, and therefore, how usable are the ideas from Massachusetts.

Skeptics have indeed raised questions. For example, were the many economic development programs established in the Dukakis administrations merely a drop in the bucket while the bucket filled to the brim by other forces? Was a liberal government merely riding a conservative wave? After all, Massachusetts benefits from defense spending, which rises under a conservative administration in Washington; and a major tax cap, Proposition 2½, which Dukakis initially opposed, was enacted while he was between terms.

Ultimately, the answer lies in examining the record, as described in detail throughout this book. The record reveals state actions and impacts that go beyond what could be attributed to tax cuts or defense spending alone. State policies made an economic boom echo in ways that brought broader benefits to the public.

Overall, the Massachusetts story demonstrates how government can invest its resources and forge the partnerships that help enterprising people create jobs. Government can be the stimulus or catalyst to magnify and multiply private sector efforts. When any government—or any leader—acts in this way, as investor and stimulator, then it is futile anyway to attempt to parcel out "credit" for economic prosperity. Instead, we must understand how the whole system worked together—business, government, labor, cities, towns, and regions. Joe Henson of Prime Computer said it best when he remarked, "The credit belongs to all of us."

Investment economics joins the politics of partnership. "Credit," for the Massachusetts comeback, then, should go to a whole complex of forces, ranging from the macroeconomic to the political to the human, including human values. There are many new ideas reflected in the Massachusetts success story—new economic development programs, new approaches to the role of government. But behind the new ideas are some very old and very important American traditions.

The best of American values combined to make Massachusetts an economic success story: *entrepreneurship along with partnership, pragmatism along with compassion.* The challenge remaining is to move from state to nation—to reinfuse national economic policy with these values.

The competitiveness of American industry in the world economy—and with it, our ability to create jobs and provide opportunity for our citizens—is at risk. The statistics paint a disturbing picture. The U.S. world market share is eroding in major industries: down to less than 10 percent of the 1965 level in electronics, down 50 percent in machine tools in the last five years, down 35 percent or more in wide-body jets. We cannot even take refuge in fantasies that our strengths will lie in services; Japan now has a greater share of the world financial services market than does the United States. Every day, foreign investment in the United States increases, while American companies seek strategic alliances with foreign companies to boost their ability to compete. Along with the trade deficit with other countries there is a perceived "quality deficit": that the once-proud "Made in U.S.A." label no longer stands for the best.

In this grim context, the lessons of Massachusetts sound a note of hope. Investment economics at the national level—promoting new enterprises, innovating in technology, educating the work force, rebuilding infrastructure, and improving prductivity and quality in existing businesses—could spark an American comeback. And the politics of partnership could ensure that all critical parties—government, business, and labor—share and implement a vision of a strong, prosperous, and compassionate America.

CHAPTER ONE

The Comeback State

It has been called the Massachusetts Miracle, but in reality there is nothing "miraculous" about it.

The remarkable turnaround in the Massachusetts economy —from basket case in 1975 to showcase in 1988—did not come about mysteriously or accidentally. The Commonwealth pursued an economic development strategy that helped shape and expand private initiative and channel natural advantages into opportunity for all its citizens.

But here is why some people call it a miracle. In barely a decade, the employment situation in Massachusetts went from depression levels to "full employment." The industry mix went from overdependence on a few sources of jobs to growing diversity. The state's fiscal condition went from record deficits to soundness and stability. And the economic climate changed from near the bottom in national rankings of the states to the top.

Jobs: From Depression to "Full Employment"

When I began my first term as governor in 1975, the nation's economy was in the depths of a recession. Massachusetts—like so many other industrial states—was in its worst economic condition since the Great Depression. We were called the New Appalachia. Abandoned textile mills and shoe factories symbolized the forces of cheap labor and new technologies that were reshaping our global economy and transforming the very economic structure of our nation. Statewide unemployment hit a high of 12.3 percent, and over 330,000 workingwomen and workingmen were without jobs. In older cities dependent on heavy manufacturing, such as Lowell, Worcester, and Fall River, unemployment rates were even higher, and there was little or no new investment.

But Massachusetts was determined to recover and rebuild. By the fall of 1978, we had 253,000 new jobs—110,000 in 1978 alone —and the state's unemployment rate had dipped below the nation's for the first time in years. A boom period of growth and diversification was under way, bringing with it a surge that lasted into 1980 and allowed Massachusetts to ride out the national recession of 1981 and 1982 with greater resilience than virtually any of her sister states.

We did not escape that national recession without pain. In the spring of 1983, over one hundred Massachusetts communities were experiencing double-digit unemployment. Since then, Massachusetts has not only bounced back a second time but achieved a level of economic success that stands as an example of what is possible for America. Annual unemployment in 1987 hit a record low—3.2 percent—the lowest of the eleven major industrial states for the fifth straight year and, by traditional economic measures, "full employment."

From 1983 through 1987, our resurgent economy created more than 400,000 new jobs and over 84,000 new businesses.

Reinvestment in our communities and our industrial base is strong and gaining. Employment in Massachusetts rose from 2.27 million in 1975 to 3 million in 1987.

Per capita personal income growth in 1987 was the nation's highest for the fourth year in a row. And better yet, the prosperity was reaching out to embrace all citizens, even those previously left out of the economic mainstream. We helped over 43,000 welfare families to move from welfare to work, and the number of families on welfare for five years or more dropped by 30 percent.

We helped to create new jobs not just around Boston, but in regional centers like Springfield, Lowell, and Taunton. In Taunton, a city we will discuss at length later in this book, unemployment fell from close to 14 percent to 2.8 percent in five years.

Strength through Diversity

In the past, the Massachusetts economy fell prey to overdependence on one or two key industries—from shoes and textiles at the turn of the century to defense contractors in the 1960s. But the Massachusetts economic boom of the 1970s and 1980s has not been driven by defense spending or by any other single industry or sector. The world may identify Massachusetts with high technology, and high techonology with defense, but the facts are otherwise. Ours is a much richer and more diverse economic tapestry.

Several analysts have tried to make the case that the central, catalytic force in Massachusetts' recent growth has been Pentagon spending. Perhaps that conclusion is tempting, for between 1980 and 1985 the real dollar value of prime defense contracts won by Massachusetts firms increased by 59 percent, and Massachusetts ranks fourth among the states in the value of her defense contracts. We're proud of the part we play in America's defense.

But the defense picture is a static one—we've ranked between fourth and sixth in contract dollars for fifteen years, and the share of the state's employment base attributable to defense spending—about 4 percent—has not changed significantly in that time. In 1985, defense represented a steady 7 percent of the gross state product—not unimportant, but not catalytic either.

Massachusetts' advantage in securing Pentagon contracts reflects our extraordinary strength in the classroom and the laboratory. There is every reason to believe that defense dollars are here because of our academic and high-tech communities, and not vice versa. In 1965, 65 percent of the state's high technology spending came from the Pentagon or NASA. By 1980, only 25 percent did, and by 1987 the percentage had declined further.

Between 1980 and 1986, defense-related employment grew by 19 percent but accounted for only 5.5 percent of this state's new jobs. During that same period of time, civilian-oriented high-technology manufacturers employed more people, created more jobs, and grew much faster.

Overall, Massachusetts' computer and electronics manufacturers, both defense- and civilian-oriented, employ over 200,000 Bay Staters and have created 100,000 new jobs in the past decade—an invaluable contribution to the state's recovery and prosperity. Yet "high tech," by this traditional definition, represents about one-fifteenth of our work force. Our so-called mature manufacturing industries employ many more workers.

And two-thirds of our workers are employed in the fast-growing service sector, which is itself highly diversified. Tourism is the state's number two industry (more people visited Quincy Market on Boston's waterfront in 1985 than Disney World). Technology-intensive business services form one of our most explosive growth categories. Our medical, financial, and educational communities employ some 600,000 in Massachusetts and become more technology-intensive every year.

If there is a useful generalization to be made about the Massachusetts economy, it is not that we are a "high-tech" state, but that we are a "high-innovation" state. Innovation has fostered diversity and is blurring the line between mature industries, high tech, and services. As we shall see, keeping innovation going is a principal focus of the Massachusetts economic strategy.

Our Fiscal House

Economic growth requires fiscal stability, and Massachusetts has put its fiscal house in order—a lesson of particular urgency to a nation facing record deficits. When I first took office in 1975, Massachusetts was a financial basket case. Our budget deficit of nearly $600 million was proportionately the largest in the nation. Property taxes were among the highest anywhere—remember our nickname, "Taxachusetts"? Our unemployment insurance fund was so deep in debt we needed federal government loans to bail us out.

Tough choices followed—including deep cuts in social welfare programs and an income tax surcharge. The choices may have cost me my reelection in 1978. But I believed then and now that tough decisions had to be made—that's what governing and leadership are about. As I told my fellow state chief executives in 1983, unlike the current federal plan to reduce the deficit, we in the statehouses do not have "a downward glide path." We had to do it in one year. With a first wave of economic recovery came a giant step toward fiscal stability—in 1979, at the end of my first term, Massachusetts enjoyed a $200 million surplus.

In 1980, the people of this state took action against high property taxes by voting for Proposition 2½, a referendum that limited local property taxes to 2½ percent of market value.

Although I had opposed the referendum, I made it clear when I ran for election in 1982 that "making Proposition 2½ work the way it was supposed to work is the most important item on the next governor's desk."

Again, tough choices had to be made. We made Proposition 2½ work by putting in place a system of predictable and generous annual revenue sharing. We committed ourselves legislatively to sharing 40 percent of the state's growth revenues each year with our cities and towns. Without this state response, Proposition 2½ could have devastated local government and destroyed the Massachusetts economic climate. Instead, we have good municipal services *and* reduced, stabilized property taxes—an economically critical combination that didn't happen by accident.

In addition to reducing the burden of property taxes, between 1983 and 1987 Massachusetts enacted 10 tax cuts, including a record cut in state income taxes triggered by a $500 million budget surplus. Unemployment insurance taxes have been cut three times. As a percentage of personal income, our state and local tax burden for individuals has dropped from one of the country's highest to thirty-fifth in the nation. The Massachusetts Taxpayers Foundation—an independent, nonprofit public-interest research group—gives the Commonwealth high marks on business taxes, noting that the business tax burden has changed from 5 percent above the national average in 1977 to 12 percent below in 1985.

How were we able to lower taxes and still maintain a compassionate level of social spending, invest in education and economic development, and pay for the expenses of government? Two crucial factors were economic growth and good management. A third was our enhanced revenue collection initiative, the Revenue Enforcement and Protection Program (REAP). Created in 1983, REAP is our nationally recognized effort to enforce our tax laws and make everyone pay his or her fair share. We added tax auditors, introduced computers, and launched an aggressive campaign to seek out and prosecute tax evaders. After we demonstrated how tough we could be, we combined this stick with the carrot of a limited amnesty period during which delinquents could pay the state what they owed—with interest—and avoid civil and criminal prosecution.

Tougher enforcement and amnesty were two reasons the program worked so well. These were matched by an even more dramatic increase in voluntary compliance. REAP raised $900 million during its first three years of operation. The system has worked so well that it has been endorsed and used by many of my fellow governors. A comparable assault on billions in unpaid federal taxes is the first lesson that federal policymakers should adopt from the Massachusetts experience.

The Business Climate: From Near-Worst to Excellence

In 1975, Fantus, the plant-location consulting firm, ranked the Massachusetts business climate forty-sixth of forty-eight states (Ronald F. Ferguson and Helen F. Ladd, "Economic Performance and Economic Development Policy in Massachusetts" [Discussion paper D86–2, JFK School of Government, Harvard University, The State, Local, and Intergovernmental Center, May 1986], 51). The "Taxachusetts" moniker was discouraging businesses from locating or expanding here and even drove some away. Entrepreneurs and executives, who require consistency and stability in government, perceived Massachusetts as "antibusiness."

Not so today. In a survey published in *Business Week* in April 1987, Massachusetts was the only state to earn an A in each of four categories on an economic development report card: economic performance; business vitality; human, financial, physical, and cultural resources; and government policy. Similarly, *INC* magazine now ranks us at or near the very top in availability of capital, state support for business development, and business growth. Economic authors from across America point to Massachusetts not only as a state whose economy is humming, but as a state where the public and private sectors are working together to keep it that way.

All in all, there has been a remarkable transformation of the image of both the state and its government. The *Boston Globe* put it this way in 1986:

> Massachusetts. It wasn't so long ago that this word was synonymous with corruption. But in those dark days, corruption was by no means the only trait in the flawed character of the state. Massachusetts was also thought to be a haven for greed, fiscal irresponsibility, cronyism, antibusiness attitudes, racial bitterness, and poor leadership. And it was sarcastically called "Taxachusetts." But that's history. Today Massachusetts is THE COMEBACK STATE. [*Boston Globe*, 5/18/86]

Using Our Strengths: An Investment Strategy

The winds of change began to blow favorably for Massachusetts because of some key strategic advantages which we enjoyed but had not begun to exploit fully. The state's 120 colleges and universities provided a critical mass of brainpower that pioneered new, knowledge-intensive technologies for growing world markets. Route 128 and the intellectual and economic communties of Boston and Cambridge provided a haven for innovation, while our world-class medical and financial centers provided a home-grown market. Venture capital had virtually been invented in Massachusetts decades earlier, making financial support accessible to a new generation of entrepreneurs.

Massachusetts had a labor force that personified the American work ethic and dozens of proud old cities and mill towns where the Industrial Revolution had flourished through generations of community strength and solidarity.

An outstanding congressional delegation, led by such national leaders as former Speaker of the House of Representatives Thomas P. O'Neill and Senator Edward Kennedy, was there to help Massachusetts tap federal funds and attention. What we lacked in natural resources we made up for in a natural environment and a reputation for cultural excellence that would make Massachusetts a place to which America could eagerly come home.

But in 1975, these advantages had not yet made much of a difference. One reason was that state government was an economic irrelevancy on its best days and an outright impediment on its worst. As a new governor, I had to take action. State government couldn't turn the Massachusetts economy around by itself. But the Commonwealth had to become a serious player, a guiding, shaping, and unifying force for change.

One thing we did right away was to make economic development a central focus of the way state government ran. I created a Development Cabinet, run by a senior policy and planning director reporting directly to me, that brought together the several cabinet secretariats whose programs had an economic impact—not only in commerce and labor, but in housing and community development, transportation, the environment, and energy.

The Development Cabinet's mission was to rethink from top to bottom how state government impacted on the Massachusetts economy, and how it *could* impact on our economy if we had a strategy and if all of our resources, public and private, were working together. Thirteen years later, in my third administration, we are still doing that.

If our efforts have one strategic watchword, it is *investment*. Broken down to its most basic nuts and bolts, Massachusetts' investment strategy has focused on three critical underpinnings of economic recovery and growth:

- Public infrastructure
- Affordable capital for business and development
- Education and training for people

Not only have we greatly expanded the state's involvement in all of these areas, but we have undertaken from the start to blend and target our investments, to fill needs and seize opportunities, and to use public dollars to leverage as much private investment as possible. In short, Massachusetts has been more than "activist" over the past thirteen years when it comes to economic development—it has been entrepreneurial.

INFRASTRUCTURE

In 1975, we began rebuilding a neglected and crumbling economic infrastructure. In an era when every major construction project poses legitimate environmental and community concerns, we planned and built interstate highways that were critical to the economic revitalization of Western, Central, and Southeastern Massachusetts. We have all but completed a $2 billion modernization and expansion of the Metropolitan Boston transit system. We have substantially rebuilt the Port of Boston and the rail freight network in Massachusetts. And we are helping local and regional governments build nearly $400 million in sewage treatment works.

The job of creating an infrastructure for the twenty-first century is far from over. More than a dozen new transportation projects of great regional significance are in the planning or early construction stages, from a long-awaited Pittsfield Airport Connector in the Berkshires to the restoration of an extensive commuter rail network south of Boston. Our legislature recently committed another $400 million for local sewage treatment facilities.

Two projects of unprecedented scale that hold the key to economic progress in metropolitan Boston and New England

are now on a firm timetable for completion in the late 1990s—
the $3.3 billion Third Harbor Tunnel, Seaport Access Road,
and reconstruction of the Central Artery; and the $2.9 billion
cleanup of Boston Harbor.

CAPITAL

It was clear a decade ago that if entrepreneurs were to invest in
our industries and developers were to invest in our cities, Massachusetts had to help. And help we did, with a series of capital
formation initiatives that have paid off handsomely. The Massachusetts Industrial Finance Agency (MIFA), created in 1978,
has now financed $4 billion in growth and 76,000 new jobs
through the issuance of industrial revenue bonds and is already
packaging taxable issues and direct loans to keep the ball rolling
after tax reform.

The Massachusetts Technology Development Corporation
(MTDC), also created in 1978, was America's first and most
successful state venture capital company and has helped forty
of this state's most creative entrepreneurs get to market.

Today these two agencies head an extraordinary array of more
than a dozen public financing tools designed to stimulate the
kinds of *private* investment Massachusetts needs—in old and
new industries, in strategic land and buildings, in commercial
centers and housing.

PEOPLE

Massachusetts invests in her people. Even a decade ago, while
concentrating on the infrastructure and capital needs of an
aging economy, we began new initiatives in education and training. Today, our commitment to education and training is paramount. Alongside the federal Job Training Partnership Act we
have placed the Bay State Skills Corporation, perhaps the na-

tion's best customized training program, and MassJobs South-east, the first of a series of regional partnerships to match private sector expansion commitments with the necessary work force.

ET Choices, our jobs program for federal Aid to Families with Dependent Children recipients, has become a national model by bringing over 43,000 welfare families into the economic mainstream, through jobs that pay on the average more than double the yearly welfare grant, at more than 8,000 Massachusetts employers.

Our reemployment assistance program has helped over 20,000 workers displaced by plant closings and layoffs face the economic challenge of their lives. Three-quarters of them have found jobs, averaging over 85 percent of their old wages.

The foundation on which any training effort must be built is education. In 1985, the Massachusetts legislature enacted a comprehensive Education Improvement Act. This bill strengthens our entire K-12 system through special state aid to poorer districts, teacher development, and a stronger curriculum.

Finally we are making Massachusetts' twenty-seven public colleges and universities into the intellectual resource they must be for this state's economic future. We have increased state support for public higher education by a percentage greater than any other industrial state in the country. Now, we are ready to undertake a $954 million, ten-year modernization and expansion of the system *and* a prepaid College Opportunity Fund that will keep tuitions affordable for tomorrow's students.

Innovation and Opportunity:
A Vision of the Future

These public investments, and the private commitments they help produce, would amount to less than the sum of their parts if we did not have a clear vision of where we want the Massachusetts economy to go. For while most decisions about which investments to make, which technologies to try, and which communities to build in are private, and are made for business reasons, the public role in shaping some of those decisions can be profoundly important. Massachusetts has set her sights on two far-reaching economic goals—*innovation* and *opportunity*.

INNOVATION

Over the last 5 years, Massachusetts has made a conscious effort to help both her mature manufacturing industries *and* her promising new technology producers gain a solid footing in the state, national, and world economies.

Based on the findings and recommendations of the Commission on the Future of Mature Industries that I appointed in 1983, we are now able to focus a full battery of resources and analytical talent on companies that have a legitimate chance to change and grow. We have had some widely reported successes, many less visible victories, and some losses. But we are in the mature industries business to stay.

Our objective is not to deny economic change. On the contrary, our objective is to help ensure that change in the form of technological, capital, and managerial innovations reaches into our older industries and fashions a competitive future for them.

At the same time, we have actively joined with businesses, educators, and venture capitalists to promote the most promising of this state's leading-edge technologies. At our Massachusetts Microelectronics Center of Excellence, our engineering schools and computer companies are training the next generation of silicon-chip engineers. In four other Centers of Excellence, creative partnerships are advancing our capabilities in biotechnology, marine sciences, photovoltaics, and polymer plastics, and bringing new ideas to market.

In 1987, we began a new agenda of initiatives to speed the process of technological innovation. We are planning a new

Center of Excellence in applied technology and productivity—
a network of "greenhouses" to help companies and workers find
the solutions to more modern, efficient manufacturing capabilities. We intend to build a series of small business incubators
across Massachusetts and to help several of our prize Massachusetts industries—from apple growers to software producers—
market their goods nationally and overseas.

The fruits of our labor to promote and advance innovation
can be seen in companies as diverse as an egg grower in Westminster and a developer of desktop publishing systems in Cambridge, a spaghetti manufacturer in Lowell and the creator of
millimeter radar technology in Amherst, a diversifying General
Electric in Pittsfield and Fitchburg and a brand-new solar cell
producer in Taunton's Myles Standish Industrial Park.

In that park, five years of hard work are paying off in dozens
of new plants and thousands of new jobs for a part of Massachusetts long in economic distress. It is precisely this convergence
of technological innovation and regional revitalization that
brings us to the second of our principal goals—economic opportunity for every citizen in every Massachusetts community.

OPPORTUNITY

In 1975, our historic downtowns were economic ghost towns,
the infrastructure and housing of our cities were in disrepair,
and urban unemployment was far higher than an already dis-
tressing statewide average.

But we rejected the conventional wisdom that our cities were
dead, and we undertook a state urban policy unlike any in
America. Starting in Lowell—the city my father had come to
from Greece seventy-five years ago—we created an urban heritage park program, and today thirteen heritage parks are open,
being built, or being planned. These are not parks in the traditional sense—they are careful, loving restorations of buildings
and canals and mills and waterfronts that celebrate the indus-

trial and ethnic histories of our cities and help pave the way for economic renewal.

We required state agencies to locate their offices and facilities in older downtowns. We used housing subsidies to rehabilitate landmark buildings. We made commercial development projects eligible for industrial revenue bonds—but only in established downtown and neighborhood business districts.

We invested in regional transit systems that focus on downtown centers; we provided the funds to help our cities build convention centers, auditoriums, parking garages, streets, sidewalks, and access roads. Why? To help our cities nail down private investment and create good jobs for their people.

We are now within sight of a goal I set over a decade ago—the revitalization of every urban center in Massachusetts. Some, like Springfield, are very far along. Others have further to go. But virtually all have put in place a critical mass of public and private investment and an all-important sense of self-renewal. And this has enabled us to broaden our view, to look beyond downtowns to neighborhoods, on one hand, and to entire regions, on the other.

One negative consequence of our economic resurgence is a serious shortage of affordable housing. The average single-family house in Massachusetts now costs $150,000, and for several years housing production fell some 20,000 units per year short of demand. With the federal government's withdrawal from the affordable housing business, Massachusetts has a major challenge on its hands.

Our response has been the Massachusetts Housing Partnership—a state-led family of over 120 local alliances of cities and towns, developers, builders, nonprofit organizations, banks, union pension funds, and neighborhood leaders. Through public contributions of land and innovative new financing programs, the partnership is producing and growing.

Our other strategy for area development is called "Targets for Opportunity." However strong the state's overall economic performance, and however powerful the economic momentum of downtown Boston and Route 128, Massachusetts still has communities and entire regions that are not sharing fully in our booming economy. Northern Berkshire County, the Northern Tier of Franklin and Worcester counties, the Blackstone Valley, and Southeastern Massachusetts need special help to move into the mainstream. Their unemployment rates—in double digits and far in excess of the statewide average in the winter of 1983 —have dropped substantially. But we have more work to do if we are going to build diversified, innovative, and durable regional economies throughout Massachusetts.

In each of these target areas, the Commonwealth has reached out to leaders of local government, business, labor, and education to help them fashion an economic strategy that they and we believe can work. The initiative and the insight come from the people of the region—but essential support and encouragement come from the state.

Massachusetts and America

There is a lesson for national policy in the Massachusetts economic experience, and it is not that everything we've tried in Massachusetts will work equally well, or even be appropriate, in other states or in the country as a whole. The lesson lies in how we have approached the job of economic development, and how our approach has made a difference where it counts—in the lives of people, companies, and communities.

In each of the next four chapters of this book, a discussion of our development policies is interwoven with case studies of Massachusetts businesses. In chapters 2 through 4, we explore how our investments in creative entrepreneurship revitalized communities, and a skilled, well-educated work force are helping Massachusetts attain her twin objectives of innovation and opportunity.

In chapter 5, we show how all of our strategic investments come together to help build strong, diverse, and durable regional economies.

Finally, in chapter 6, we draw on all these lessons to outline a new kind of economic strategy for the nation—one that is both concrete and caring, one that sees beyond statistics to the people and places that need economic growth and are ready to make it happen.

CHAPTER TWO

Today's Entrepreneurs, Tomorrow's Technologies: Investments in Innovation

In today's competitive global economy, economic success rests on the power of innovation. Innovation means new ideas successfully brought into use—ideas that are developed and applied by entrepreneurs seeking to create new economic value. This is what we find at the heart of the remarkable comeback in Massachusetts. Believing in the power of their ideas, entrepreneurs started new businesses and expanded and revitalized old ones, through new technologies or better ideas for producing and marketing their wares. The world wanted the fruits of these new technologies, and the entrepreneurial explosion that resulted turned parts of our state into an enormous job-creation machine. Public-private partnerships, in which public resources helped fuel private initiative, kept the machine working.

Massachusetts has long been fertile ground for new ideas and the technology they spawn. By 1776, the American concept of freedom had germinated here and been tested in Lexington and

Concord. In the nineteenth century, Donald McKay's clipper ships took American goods across the world. In the Industrial Revolution, large-scale textile looms were conceived in Waltham and developed in Lowell. The computer revolution sprang from the laboratories of MIT and Harvard. Today, Massachusetts is at the forefront of emerging technologies like electronic publishing, biotechnology, artificial intelligence, photovoltaics, fiber optics, marine sciences, and polymers.

Behind each of these technologies are people with the energy and tools to capitalize on new ideas. For example, when I gave the state's first four Innovation Awards in 1987, Kenneth Olsen was honored for founding and building Digital Equipment Corporation in Maynard—a company that began in an old mill and is now second in size only to IBM in its industry.

In short, lacking the geographer's measures of natural resources—rich soil, abundant energy, moderate climate, and proximity to markets—Massachusetts has thrived on a natural resource of another sort: the intelligence and creativity of our people. "Yankee ingenuity" has created new ideas, crafted innovative ways to implement them, and brought about a better life. The question for state government was how to ensure that the ideas kept flowing, that the ingenuity continued to be translated into ventures that created jobs.

Ten years ago, most states were barely involved in economic development. At best, they had traditional commerce departments and traditionally narrow economic agendas—promote, recruit, and cut taxes for new business. But in the last decade, most states have taken a much broader view of economic development and assumed a catalytic role in the process. States are large and inclusive enough to have a real economic impact, but close enough to the grass roots to tailor their activities. States can be especially responsive to entrepreneurs and communities, anticipating and supporting change, encouraging and supporting innovation. In Massachusetts, we embraced this activist role and made innovation a central theme in state policies.

The best way to support innovation, I recognized, was to help entrepreneurs get the resources they need to develop new ideas and turn them into practical realities. Because financial resources are one of the fundamental "power tools" driving entrepreneurship, we started there.

Accelerating Capital Formation for Business Development

It was clear from the beginning that we needed more than just a single program if we were to use public investment to stimulate and reinforce private investment. One or two tools would not be enough to respond to the variety of needs we saw. Analysts Neal Peirce and Carol Steinbach described our commitment this way in the *National Journal*:

> No other state government has created as many economic development tools as the Bay State under Dukakis. Some seek to assist burgeoning high-tech firms, others to bolster mature industries, others to assist housing and community development in distressed areas. The money involved ranges from a few million dollars to the Massachusetts Capital Resources Corporation, a $100 million business loan fund that Dukakis induced the insurance industry to finance in exchange for a break on its state tax obligations. [*National Journal*, 5/25/85]

We tried, then, to deliver one major focus of this commitment involving the ability to deliver a *package* of financing alternatives to businesses, tailor-made to their particular circumstances.

At the heart of the package is the Massachusetts Industrial Finance Agency (MIFA). From its creation in my first administration through 1988, MIFA has approved industrial development bonds for more than 1,700 business expansions in Massachusetts. Approximately 76,000 new jobs were created as a result of these financings, and the impact on industrial innovation has been sweeping. Hundreds of mature manufacturers have retooled with MIFA mortgages. But MIFA financing also provided Integrated Genetics, a six-year-old biotechnology company in Framingham, with the $3 million it needed to pioneer a rapid detection test for salmonella and become a leader in the cloning of animal fertility hormones.

While federal tax changes have cut deeply into MIFA's volume of tax-exempt industrial development bonds, the agency has created new financing programs that keep Massachusetts in the forefront of creative assistance for business. In 1984, MIFA secured legislation expanding its mortgage insurance capability into a full-blown guaranteed loan program for small industrial firms. A 1987 law has given MIFA the power and flexibility it needs to assemble taxable financing pools in the hundreds of millions of dollars and place them in the Euromarket, with the state's pension investment fund, or wherever the state's business expansion needs can get the best deal.

No other state can offer its entrepreneurs the financing capabilities embodied in MIFA, but there's much more. The Massachusetts Capital Resources Corporation was formed in 1978 with $100 million in funding by nine Massachusetts life insurance companies in exchange for tax relief, as a way to provide high-risk capital for manufacturing companies unable to obtain financing from conventional sources. The Thrift Institutions Fund for Economic Development was created by the legislature in 1984. In exchange for an adjustment in the state's tax treatment of her savings banks, those 272 banks set up a $100 million pool to participate in loans originated by MIFA and several other state finance agencies.

The Thrift Fund is a good example of how to leverage public investment, because it combined its money with that of other agencies. As Chairwoman Paula Gold, the Commonwealth's secretary of consumer affairs and business regulation recalled,

"We quickly decided to tie in with what already existed. That decision got us off the ground quickly." The fifteen-member board (eight bankers and seven public officials) selected as the first loan recipients just the kind of diverse cross section of industries we were trying to help: a paper box company, a scissors manufacturer, and a fishing operation. All had been unable to obtain full financing from conventional sources.

The financing of ChemDesign Corporation is a classic example of how the state's multiple forms of investment work together—and an equally classic success story of an American entrepreneur.

INVESTING IN CHEMICALS: AN AMERICAN TALE

ChemDesign Corporation founder and CEO Richard E. Brooks was the son of a Boston police detective who realized his boyhood dream of joining the Boston Celtics of the National Basketball Association. After a very brief stay, Coach Red Auerbach advised him to move from the NBA to an MBA. His return to school for the business degree led him to a twenty-year stint at Polaroid, but he eventually became frustrated working in a large corporate bureaucracy—tired of "the corporate minuet," as he put it. He dreamed of starting his own company. In 1981, he left Polaroid to round up the capital and the managerial team—including other big-company managers from Polaroid, Upjohn, and Syntex—to form ChemDesign, a developer and producer of sophisticated pharmaceuticals and specialty chemicals.

In December 1983, Massachusetts celebrated the groundbreaking ceremonies for ChemDesign's new $4.5 million facility in Fitchburg. Located in the city-owned 231 Industrial Park, the plant includes a two-story building, a chemical production operation housed behind specially constructed safety walls, and a lovely park area. Brooks insisted that the site be left as natural as possible; instead of a building surrounded by sod, his headquarters is surrounded by natural boulders and mature trees. This is consistent with the company's written "social objectives," which include promoting meaningful and fulfilling employment.

ChemDesign's operations began in late 1984, and by 1987 sales had quadrupled to about $25 million. An office expansion and new warehouse added in 1986 were signs of the company's rapid growth and success. Brooks expects the current work force of fifty to increase by an additional thirty to thirty-five technical and professional jobs by the end of 1988. Providing a payroll in excess of $2.5 million, these jobs are an important contribution to the revitalization of Greater Fitchburg, one of our Targets for Opportunity where unemployment had exceeded the state average.

ChemDesign's experience is a classic model of how to blend state, federal, and private funds to create jobs and enhance the economic climate. Of the $10 million Brooks initially raised for ChemDesign, about $3 million came from MIFA-backed industrial bonds and $2 million from loans representing the investment of other public resources.

A host of state and federal programs supported the construction of the 10,000-square-feet, two-story headquarters and production plant. With strong support from the city of Fitchburg, then-Senator Paul Tsongas, and U.S. Representative Edward Boland, Fitchburg and ChemDesign were awarded a $625,000 low-interest HUD Urban Development Action Grant (UDAG) loan. On the state level, the Massachusetts Capital Resources Corporation (MCRC) committed over $1 million to the project. The Massachusetts Community Development Finance Corporation (CDFC), in conjunction with the Fitchburg Cleghorn Neighborhood Development Corporation, also provided $250,000 in equity and loan financing.

The "early-in-the-project" commitment of funding from CDFC, UDAG, and MCRC helped ChemDesign leverage other funds and loans. A creative local bank, U.S. Trust/Boston, purchased $1.1 million in industrial revenue bonds and granted a $650,000 building loan as part of a Small Business Administration (SBA) loan package. More funds came from the Massachusetts Business Development Corporation. MBDC helped ChemDesign obtain another SBA-guaranteed $500,000 loan at attractive rates.

Coupled with private equity from the principals and local investors, these state and federal funds allowed ChemDesign to successfully offer a $3 million private equity placement through a major New York investment banking firm. With total capital of about $10 million, the company was positioned to close the Fitchburg deal as well as complete a leveraged buyout of an existing specialty chemical firm in Wisconsin, renamed SpecialtyChem. Since commencing operations in late 1984, the company has formed an additional subsidiary, CheMarketing International, which exports ChemDesign's products worldwide.

Financial investment from the state paid off for Brooks not only in supplying the resources he needed to get started but also in providing another form of support—a sign of confidence, a legitimacy to the venture that helped his entrepreneurial team attract other funds and maintain their own enthusiasm for the venture.

If ChemDesign represents new industrial technologies in the Greater Fitchburg economy, nearby Westminster Farms is the rural opposite. Yet both businesses show how public resources can aid the development of new technology in any industry, new or old. And both show how government investment can give an additional boost to an entrepreneur with a vision.

NEWFANGLED MACHINES, OLD-FASHIONED CHICKENS

Westminster Farms is the largest and most highly automated egg producer in Massachusetts. It is located off a long, steep country road in Westminster, a small rural town next to Fitchburg. To the right is a one-story office building. Attached and to the left for hundreds of feet are the six chicken coops, home to over half a million chickens.

The production floor is a marvel of modern machinery and production management. First, the coops: cages with six hens each are stacked four or five high and extend down the row out of sight. The eggs roll into a conveyer leading to the perpendicular junction of the larger conveyer, then onto the packaging floor. There are small, mostly white feathers everywhere, on the ground and floating in the air. The slow moving conveyer is dotted, not capacity-filled, with brown eggs. Every now and then one can spot a broken egg on the floor of the coop or along the conveyer.

As the eggs go into the production room they are first dipped in a solution and washed by a spray shower. They are quickly blown-heat dried, then candled. A young man looks for cracked or otherwise unacceptable eggs, removing the offenders. The eggs continue to a "weighing station" which automatically sends each egg to the proper column for packaging. Operators load the egg cartons at each station. The cartons are stacked on carts and then carried into a cooled, partitioned section of the cement shop floor for storage.

Westminster Farms was started in Billerica in 1952. Founder and owner John Ricca eventually added twenty-three other locations in neighboring Maine and New Hampshire. Seeking to achieve economies of scale through consolidation, Ricca decided to move the company and its coops to Westminster in 1984. As vice president of the United Cooperative Farmers, an area agribusiness group, Ricca had learned from representatives of the Massachusetts Department of Agriculture that the state could provide industrial revenue bond financing through the Massachusetts Industrial Finance Agency for the construction and machinery costs of his new business plan.

The staff of MIFA assisted Ricca in every step of the process. The facility was built with a $4 million MIFA mortgage. In addition, the farm obtained a $500,000 SBA loan and $740,000 as leases for equipment from a local bank. The result is that Westminster Farms is now not only the largest egg production facility in Massachusetts but also the fifth largest in New England.

Ricca toured the United States and Europe in order to learn about the newest egg production technologies. As a result, he installed the present highly automated processing and production facility. The system includes a computerized egg counter which controls the egg traffic and speed of the conveyers, as well as the mechanized sorter. Similar systems exist in the Midwest, but nowhere else in New England.

The company can now package 200 cases per hour (or 72,000 eggs) instead of 70 cases previously. Also, the farm has achieved economies in transportation by completely eliminating the previous routine in which eggs were produced in the twenty-three sites and transported to Billerica for packaging. The eggs are now shipped fresher, faster, and cheaper.

Westminster Farms exists in a very competitive environment and has a 5 percent share of the market in Massachusetts, mostly in the eastern area. Eager for a bigger share of the egg business, Ricca is particularly enthusiastic about the state's incentives in the area of marketing. For example, the company has been helped a great deal by the new state Massachusetts Seal program, whose slogan and symbol, printed on Massachusetts' products, is "Massachusetts Grown—and Fresher." Marketing presents the greatest challenge facing the company in the future, because, as Ricca commented, "egg consumption is at a standstill because of health concerns."

The state has also been supportive in other ways. For example, the company was able to take advantage of technical assistance with computer programming for flock record-keeping by the University of Massachusetts Extension Services Program. To improve the access road to his new facility, Ricca entered into a partnership with the state. He paid $15,000 for the engineering work, and the state is building the road. In the spring of '86, the state spent $17,000 on a marketing study which considered the feasibility and value of a composting operation in Fitchburg. With encouraging results in hand, Ricca is now planning to enter the second stage of growth by building a composting operation that will help solve a significant environmental landfill problem in Massachusetts. _____

Westminster Farms, like ChemDesign and many other businesses, benefited from our efforts to use the kinds of grants and loans in this state's toolkit of financial alternatives.

But we want to do still more. We want to help boost entrepreneurs at the critical point where risk capital would make a difference in whether the business ever got started. For this we needed an innovation of our own.

Innovation in Finance: State Venture Capital for Technology Entrepreneurs

In 1978 we created the Massachusetts Technology Development Corporation (MTDC), the nation's first state-financed venture capital corporation for new technology start-ups. MTDC's goal was to act like any other venture capitalist, with an eye toward a moneymaking portfolio built on bankable undertakings. But by accepting somewhat more marginal projected returns, the MTDC—which always invests in conjunction with private venture capitalists—provides needed capital for entrepreneurs that might not otherwise be available.

By the time MTDC began operating in 1979, the reduction in the federal capital gains tax in 1978 had helped to stimulate a significant increase in venture capital funds. As private capital flourished in the early 1980s, MTDC focused its investment activity on start-up companies where a "capital gap" existed. Despite the increased availability of venture capital funding, venture capitalists have tended to avoid early-stage start-ups—investors with commercially unproven innovations. The MTDC, with an interest in developing new technologies rather than receiving high returns, stepped in to bridge the capital gap by supplying qualified companies with the cash to develop their products to the stage at which they could attract larger, fully private venture financing.

Since MTDC's policy is to complement, not compete with, private financial institutions, every dollar MTDC has invested in early-stage technology companies based in Massachusetts has helped raise an additional $5.50 in private coinvestment funds. Clearly, state backing helped mitigate the apparent financial risk in the eyes of other financial institutions. MTDC's investments have generated well over $50 million in funding from private sources—and have created over two thousand jobs in the state.

The typical MTDC investment is $100,000 to $300,000, while most private capitalists prefer not to bother with deals under $1 million. While the management and composition of MTDC's portfolio has changed, the agency continues to pursue four basic objectives:

- To help create primary employment in technology-based industries in Massachusetts
- To attract and leverage private investment in Massachusetts companies
- To foster the application of technological innovation where the state's companies are, or can be, leaders
- To nurture entrepreneurship among Massachusetts citizens, planting the seeds for long-term economic development

From the beginning, MTDC recognized that implementing these goals would require more than money. The Management Assistance and Financial Packaging programs act as consulting services to entrepreneurs. Through the Management Assistance Program, MTDC staff members review business plans and recommend a plan for raising the necessary capital, considering both private and public sources. The Financial Packaging Program assists entrepreneurs with technologically innovative products but little proven track record, to develop the best method for presenting the investment opportunity to private investors.

MTDC strives to be as innovative as those individuals it was established to assist. Bureaucracy does not stifle entrepreneurs; no preprinted application forms frighten them off. Instead, entrepreneurs bring a written business plan to the MTDC. Just as conventional venture capitalists would do when reviewing the business plan, MTDC looks for the answers to a number of critical questions about projected share of the market. But it also asks the most important questions from the standpoint of the citizens of the state: What employment or other economic benefits will Massachusetts receive? Is the product truly innovative? Does the company really need this financing? In short, why should MTDC make the investment?

With these guidelines in mind, the MTDC staff has sifted through two hundred business plans since 1979. To date forty companies have been funded, with twenty-nine still in the MTDC portfolio. Of the eleven companies in the portfolio, several are no longer in business, as is expected in the venture capital environment, for new ventures always carry high risks. But in fact, MTDC has had a rate of business failures much lower than typical venture capitalists, due, in part, to the counseling they give to start-ups.

The few business failures are more than offset by the success of the other companies no longer in the MTDC portfolio. Those have become public corporations and have provided the state with a substantial return on the initial investment. Spire Corporation, MTDC's very first venture, was a still-young photovoltaics company in 1979. In 1984, Spire was an industry leader, a public company, and a big winner for MTDC. The proceeds, of course, are available for reinvestment in new ventures.

A glance at a recent MTDC portfolio (following) shows an exciting array of new ventures with promising technologies—technologies that can not only create tomorrow's jobs but also contribute to innovations in mature industries.

The MTDC Portfolio

Company	Location	Industry	MTDC Investment	Initial Investment Date
ACCESS TECHNOL-OGY, INC.	Natick	Business Software	$250,000	11/83
AEONIC SYSTEMS, INC.	Billerica	Process Control	250,000	1/84
AMCARD SYSTEMS, INC.	Hudson	Card Reader/Photo Identification	200,000	1/84
AMDEV, INC.	Haverhill	Medical Instruments	250,000	12/83
ASECO CORPORATION	Marlboro	Automation: Semiconductor	250,000	3/84
ASPEN TECHNOLOGY, INC.	Cambridge	Chemical Process Simulation	150,000	12/81
BUSINESS RESEARCH CORP.	Boston	On-line Computer Database	210,000	8/83
CAMBRIDGE ANALYTICAL ASSOCIATES, INC.	Boston	Hazardous & Toxic Waste Analysts	200,000	3/85
CGX CORPORATION	Acton	CAD/CAM Work-stations	275,000 *	8/82
CHROMATIC TECH-NOLOGIES, INC.	Franklin	Specialty Fiber Optic Cabling	250,000	6/85
COMPUTER SOLU-TIONS, INC.	Burlington	Manufacturing Software	300,000 *	7/83
CRYSTAL SYSTEMS, INC.	Salem	Materials Science	250,000	10/81
DISPLAY COMPO-NENTS, INC.	Westford	Video Display Deflector Yokes	295,000 *	1/80
FOTEC, INC.	Boston	Fiber Optic Test Equipment	325,000 *	6/83
GEOGRAPHIC SYSTEMS, INC.	Andover	Mapping Software	280,000 *	2/85
ICON CORPORATION	Cambridge	Automation: Factory	389,000 *	12/80
INTERLEAF, INC.	Cambridge	Publishing Software	200,000	8/82
LASER ENGINEERING, INC.	Waltham	Laser Technology	125,000	3/83
MICROTOUCH SYSTEMS, INC.	Woburn	Touch Screen Products	250,000	9/86
OPTICAL MICRO SYSTEMS, INC.	Danvers	Ophthalmic Instruments	200,000	11/83
PRACTEK ASSOCIATES, INC.	Chicopee	Educational Communications	225,000 *	7/83
PROCOMICS IN-TERNATIONAL, INC.	Woburn	Automation: Semiconductor	150,000	7/82
PUBLISHING TECHNOLOGY, CORP.	Needham	List Management Software	25,000	5/82

RANDWAL INSTRU- MENTS, INC.	Southbridge	Ophthalmic Instruments	204,000*	12/82
SKY COMPUTERS, INC.	Lowell	Array Processors	250,000	8/82
VITRONICS CORPORATION	Newburyport/ Newmarket, NH	Infra-red Technology	100,000	5/83
XYLOGICS, INC.	Burlington	Disc Controllers	362,500*	4/80
ZOOM TELEPHONICS, INC.	Boston	Telecommunications	200,000	8/85

* Includes subsequent rounds of investment

INVESTING IN INTERLEAF: HIGH TECH, HIGH PAYOFF

The high stakes venture capital game MTDC is playing is intended to have equally high payoffs. The Interleaf experience proves this can be done. By 1986, the $200,000 MTDC had invested in Interleaf in 1982 was worth $2.5 million. That's a return on investment that's hard to match—even in the thriving Cambridge high-tech community where Interleaf resides.

Two years earlier, in 1984, MTDC had sold off about two-thirds of its investment in Interleaf for a profit of about $500,000. And the remaining two-thirds was worth about $2 million when Interleaf made its first public stock offering in 1986. Once the initial investment had accomplished MTDC's goal—promoting the formation of new high-tech companies to create new jobs—the state was prepared to sell, liquidating in order to make other investments with the $2 million—"hopefully in another Interleaf," as MTDC told the press.

Interleaf is a young firm that designs, develops, and markets a turnkey desktop publishing system for the advanced processing power of a new generation of commercial computers—the extremely fast 32-bit processor. The Interleaf system allows an individual to compose, edit, and publish photo-ready copy illustrated by graphs and photos for manuals, reports, and proposals. In the past it has been necessary to contract out for design, layout, typesetting, and photoproofing—a process which often involved two or more separate enterprises. The Interleaf Electronic Publishing System gives the composer immediate and total control over the final product, saving up to 50 percent of the time and expense.

Interleaf was a forward-thinking venture. In 1981 David Boucher and his cofounder Harry George foresaw the market in computer-based publishing, but their business plan did not impress venture capitalists. At a meeting in New York, one potential investor reportedly started to fall asleep during a presentation of the Interleaf proposal.

Unsuccessful in their quest for venture capital backing, Boucher and George turned to MTDC. MTDC immediately grasped Interleaf's market philosohy; the cofounders received $200,000 from the MTDC over the course of a year, adding $50,000 in personal savings. Interleaf was up and running. Twelve months later Interleaf produced its first successful public product demonstration. Interleaf began shipping product in 1984, and within a year customers like Boeing and American Can had snapped up $8.3 million in Interleaf systems. Between 1983 and 1986, the company grew from 20 to 325 people, an extraordinary growth that was both foreseen and managed, and by 1986 Interleaf had garnered $41 million from a public offering and from private venture capital investors, including Eastman Kodak. In fiscal 1986, Interleaf posted revenues of $18.6 million and expected to see them double the next year. Its new headquarters in the midst of Cambridge's "software city-within-a-city" near MIT is an inviting setting for potential customers and visitors to experiment with uses of Interleaf products.

INVESTING IN TOMORROW'S TECHNOLOGIES: STRATEGIES FOR "IDEA FORMATION"

Financing tools are important—but not enough. For government to help provide the capital to power innovation is an important step. But it is only one step. To take only a financial view of entrepreneurship and innovation is inherently limited. All the money in the world to support new businesses and new technologies will not mean a thing unless the *ideas* for innovation are there in the first place.

Furthermore, helping finance business innovation efforts one by one, through investments in individual companies, needs to be augmented by investments in the development of entire industries. This is increasingly recognized by experts on the economy. For example, the National Cooperative Research Act of 1984 loosened antitrust restrictions to allow joint development by companies in the same industry through the prototype stage. By 1986, at least forty industrywide research-and-development consortia had been organized nationwide, sponsored by industry groups as diverse as computer firms and glass manufacturers, making clear that the ideas, the technology, behind innovation often require a critical mass beyond the capacity of any one company.

We conceived the Massachusetts Centers of Excellence Program as one means for giving a boost to innovation at the industry level. Through these centers we would assemble and cluster the building blocks for business formation and technology development in critical industries—and then fill in the gaps. The centers are a concept and a focus of attention as much as a physical place, though they also reflect geographic specialization. By 1987 five centers were in place, with a sixth—in applied technology—in the planning stages.

The Centers of Excellence illustrate how government can be more than a passive investor—how government can also take an active role in helping innovators and innovations emerge and succeed. Just as MTDC supported Spire Corporation's expansion as a single photovoltaics producer, the Photovoltaics Center of Excellence is supporting the development of the photovoltaics industry as a whole.

In a certain sense, Boston's Route 128 was the state's first "center of excellence." Along that well-known highway, and at nearby MIT and other key institutions, were found the tools innovators need to develop and commercialize new computer-related technologies. These range from academic institutions for research and a supply of technical talent to venture capital sources interested in the computer industry to the likelihood that so many companies doing similar things would learn from each other and develop the market for their products.

Route 128—like California's Silicon Valley—took years to develop "naturally." And America was lucky to have such centers evolve. But in today's highly competitive global economy, with other countries investing in their own Silicon Glens and Silicon Bogs, we cannot afford to wait; we need to speed up the process of creating the conditions for concentrations of technology and business development to occur.

The Centers of Excellence Program reflected a bet that we could nurture those conditions elsewhere in the state, for other growing industries that could be tomorrow's hot technologies. Each center would assess what that industry already had going for it, trying to leverage strengths and shore up weaknesses. Each would expand and accelerate partnerships that already exist between the entrepreneurial and academic communities, drawing on the full range of state economic development resources.

The Centers of Excellence represented the conjunction of *technology* and *place*. The strategy for developing centers was twofold:

1. Unite business, academic, and government leaders around a particular *technology*.
2. Locate or create a "flagship" *facility* to serve as the rallying point for the center. They should be in places where the technology is already rooted and should be designed to serve the problems unique to that technology and region.

The first five Centers of Excellence reflect this blend:

- Microelectronics, an obvious choice given Massachusetts' concentration of computer firms and the competitive threat from other states and overseas, headquartered at a new technology park west of Boston
- Polymer plastics at the University of Massachusetts—Amherst, a logical choice given the school's preeminence in polymer sciences, the thriving plastics industry nearby, and a new General Electric advanced plastics research complex under development thirty miles to the west in Pittsfield
- Marine sciences at Southeastern Massachusetts University, to advance a critical mass of activities that relate to the sea, from the exploration of the oceans to commercial aquaculture to marine engineering;
- Biotechnology at the University of Massachusetts Medical School at Worcester and its new Biomedical Research Park;
- And photovoltaics—Spire Corporation's industry—in Greater Boston.

On October 8, 1985, at a ceremony in Boston's Computer Museum, I swore in forty-five directors of the Centers of Excellence. Evelyn Murphy, then secretary of economic affairs and now my lieutenant governor, chaired the board of a new state agency, the Massachusetts Centers of Excellence Corporation, designed to provide the overall guidance for center activities. This agency was designed to focus on the future more than the present—a future to be based on a diverse economy of new-product technologies as well as traditional industries that could be made more competitive by the application and transfer of new process technologies. The MCEC had a special fund to support research activities for which other resources are not available. Two $1 million rounds of MCEC research grants have been awarded.

Each Center of Excellence was built on investments the state had already made. And so, when the Photovoltaics Center of Excellence was established, Roger Little of the MTDC-financed Spire Corporation was a key.

ENERGY FROM THE SUN: POWERING THE PHOTOVOLTAICS INDUSTRY

Massachusetts is a global focal point of the photovoltaics indus-try, and Spire is among the leading turnkey photovoltaics equip-ment manufacturing companies. Spire's CEO, Roger Little, says that Spire's job is to put other people in the photovoltaics busi-ness. He wants the company to become the "McDonalds of solar cells," a vision that is a long way from the one he had in 1969 when he founded Spire to do consulting and research on energy beams and particle physics for the aerospace industry.

By 1978, Spire had developed new manufacturing technolo-gies for the solar cells used on spacecraft, and when the oil em-bargo opened the "terrestrial" market to photovoltaics, the company was already a leader in designing manufacturing tech-nologies and equipment. Spire was ready to move into the field of alternative energy when other forces intervened. As the solar-cell market developed, Roger Little watched as large oil compa-nies took over the cell-manufacturing end of the business, as federal R & D support for the fledgling industry ebbed under the Reagan adminstration, and as the giant Japanese electronic firms entered the fray. Little decided that, while his company was too small to compete directly with the giants, he could outflank them all by selling what none of them was interested in selling: the production skills, manufacturing equipment, technology, and supplies.

To implement this strategy, Little developed a network of joint-venture partners, allowing Spire at times to work behind protec-tive tariff barriers. The company sells the equipment, training, and raw materials to partners in developing countries who in turn create their own photovoltaic industries. When a plant goes into business, Spire then supplies the solar cells from which the modules are made. Later, as the local market expands to support other small plants, Spire will sell to the partnership the unprocessed silicon wafers from which the cells are made.

While working to develop this network of joint-venture partners, Little has kept Spire in the contract research business, not only bringing in revenues in the form of research grants, but also keeping the company on its technical toes. Little is aware that technological obsolescence is a major threat, and that "the core innovation at Spire is its ability to adapt and change constantly." He therefore took the company into two other major fields, electronics and metal surface modification. He now operates a "portfolio" firm: operating in three different markets with complementary growth rates and cycles spreads risk, creates new opportunities, and, above all, creates an environment conducive to innovation.

In 1979 Spire was a small company, generating less than $5 million in annual sales. Despite its size, however, the MTDC recognized Spire as a leader in the emerging photovoltaics technology field. The timely infusion of capital from MTDC allowed Spire to build the momentum it needed.

One of Little's strategies is to establish "technology linkages," applying advanced process technology to new industries. New products share and build on the common technology base of the company but are targeted for different markets. For instance, Spire has developed an ion implantation process that is used principally to make solar cells at a high speed. In a specific application of this process, Spire has developed a process that improves the biocompatibility of implanted medical devices. The process has been applied to the treatment of orthopedic implants, such as hip and knee joints, and results have shown that significant improvement in the wear performance of these devices can be achieved with ion implantation.

To nonscientists, the labs are often the most impressive part of Spire. Because they require a sterile environment, visitors are not allowed to enter, instead viewing the equipment through glass windows. It is complex and futuristic—to one visitor "a step into the next century."

Little maintains that "the people resources which are available for high-tech companies are incredible." This is the main benefit Spire derives from being based in Massachusetts. All its suppliers are in the state and Spire is also able to benefit from the support of twelve outside machine shops and from the proximity of Harvard and MIT. The universities provide the company with a source of talent; Spire also has relationships with individual professors with whom they consult when writing proposals. These relationships are invaluable to a company such as Spire.

In 1984 Little brought Spire into the public market, raising $6 million to fuel its own growth and giving a handsome return to the state for MTDC's initial investment in Spire's stock. This return will enable the MTDC to make further investments in high-technology start-ups without further burdens to the state.

For technology-based companies like Spire to continue to flourish, both the technology and the market for it must also continue to develop. So the state needed to look beyond its investment in individual companies to see how industrywide innovation could be accelerated.

Joining Roger Little on the board of directors of the Photovoltaics Center of Excellence are such industry leaders as John Fan, the young entrepreneur behind Kopin Corporation; Congressman Chester Atkins; William Hogan, president of the University of Lowell; and representatives of Harvard, MIT, and the state. Sharon Pollard, Massachusetts energy secretary, serves as chair. As Little said, "The agenda of the photovoltaics center is a result of many, many discussions with the photovoltaics industry, so it represents our thinking."

The production of photovoltaic cells to convert sunlight directly into electricity is still a small industry, under $100 million, but Massachusetts companies have a major share of the world market. In 1983, for example, Massachusetts companies, with total sales of $30.3 million, held 51 percent of the U.S. market and 28 percent of the world market. But staying on top of the technology will be increasingly important as the industry grows to a projected $4.3 billion by the end of the century. Growth is likely to be most dramatic in the developing world, where large populations and important industrial sites are isolated from electric power grids. Already there is a large overseas market. Thus, one of the most important industry needs involves worldwide marketing.

Using a combination of federal and state resources, the Commonwealth announced in 1985 the Photovoltaics Center at Boston's Logan Airport, one arm of the Center of Excellence. The building had its official opening celebration in March 1986. The center was commissioned to provide export assistance—generating market leads, helping promote products, and smoothing the way to foreign sales. Director Jane Weissman heads a staff of six that includes a marketing officer, who identifies overseas projects, and a finance officer, who identifies import-export financing assistance for both the customers (largely foreign governments) and Massachusetts firms.

The center is located in the Mass Tech Center opposite the Eastern-Continental terminal building. Exhibited in a mini-science-museum style are displays that explain the technology of photovoltaics; building the market means educating people about what the technology is and what it can do. The center customizes its presentations; for example, in preparing for a recent potential customer from the Cape Verde Islands, the staff researched that country and discovered that the drinking water supply was a major problem. When the visitor arrived, he was greeted with plans for PV applications in a desalination plant. Visitors to the center—almost two thousand in the first year—include ministers of argriculture and health from foreign governments. To further help make the technology real for people, the New England Electric System recently inaugurated a large-scale demonstration of residential PV utilization in the city of Gardner.

The second major arm of the Photovoltaics Center of Excellence is at the University of Lowell. The Massachusetts photovoltaics industry already enjoyed an important research-and-development relationship with MIT, and thus did not need a dedicated campus facility for product development, but it did need an academic resource for training. Because many PV companies were clustered northwest of Boston, Lowell made sense as a base for specialized training, particularly to help service their customers.

The Photovoltaics Center of Excellence and its board are also there to ensure that individual efforts to start and expand PV companies in Massachusetts receive priority attention from state development agencies—a commitment begun with MTDC's original sponsorship of Spire. "Sooner or later the PV technology will be applied," Director Weissman predicted. "It would be nicer to have it made in Massachusetts than 'Made in Japan.' "

The Photovoltaics Center of Excellence is designed around the needs of its industry and the particular resources that exist in the area. The Biotechnology Center of Excellence in Worcester also shows how a true center can develop out of an amalgam of unconnected resources and how partnerships between scientists and entrepreneurs can flourish in this environment.

SAVING LIVES AND SAVING JOBS: SCIENTISTS AND ENTREPRENEURS IN A BIOTECHNOLOGY PARTNERSHIP

In 1981, the business and academic leaders of Worcester had an idea—to turn seventy acres of surplus state land adjoining the University of Massachusetts Medical School into a campus park devoted to research, development, and commercialization of biomedical technologies. Worcester was already home to an important biomedical research community, and the nonprofit Worcester Business Development Corporation had a proven track record in developing industrial parks.

Today the Worcester Biomedical Research Park is a reality. The necessary land disposition procedures—including legislative authorization to sell the property on favorable terms—were completed by the summer of 1983. In 1985 the Commonwealth provided the funds for a major upgrading of the city streets leading to the park and to a $1 million grant to help fund the on-site roads and utilities.

The effort has begun to pay off. The first building was dedicated last year—and with the help of a state loan, Cambridge Biosciences, Inc., one of the state's most promising biotech firms, announced that its new headquarters would become the anchor tenant. The next major step is the development of an Innovation Center—a highly specialized shared incubation facility for small start-up ventures.

The Biotech Park will mean as many as three thousand knowledge-based jobs for Greater Worcester. But with the help of the Biotechnology Center of Excellence board, the Worcester facility also becomes the centerpiece of a much broader strategy to make Massachusetts a world leader in biotechnology during the critical next decade of this young industry's emergence.

If this strategy succeeds, it will be because of scientists dedicated to saving lives, working in partnership with entrepreneurs who create jobs. Biohybrid Technologies is just that kind of partnership.

Dr. William Chick of the Diabetes Research Program at UMass —Worcester, and Jack Hayes, a self-employed venture capitalist who holds a Harvard MBA, started Biohybrid together in 1986. Their partnership has been an extraordinarily successful one, marked by each man's unusual respect for the other's very different abilities. To Hayes, Dr. Chick represents the finest in medical research, while Hayes supplies for Dr. Chick the business expertise a physician would be hard pressed to find the time to develop.

Dr. Chick is the director of the Diabetes Center, one of twelve nationally designated endocrine research centers. His research on diabetes and the insulin-producing cells in the pancreas began in the 1970s. In the course of his fifteen years of research, Chick developed a technique to isolate the 1 to 2 percent of cells in the pancreas that produce insulin. He also developed an implant device that is surgically connected to one artery and one vein. Biohybrid was formed to commercialize this device.

The challenges that Dr. Chick has faced in trying to bring the artificial pancreas to market illustrate the needs a Center of Excellence fulfills. First, the capital requirements for the commercialization of his concept are estimated at $50 million, but no federal funds were available, and the university was unequipped to provide either the funding or the researchers necessary to complete the work. Second, the Federal Drug Administration's testing of the device had to be preceded by animal testing conducted by Dr. Chick; this would take two to three years. Third, production techniques would be needed to carry the device from the laboratory to a manufacturing setting. Finally, the product's marketing problems would have to be addressed.

Recruiting qualified researchers is a multifaceted problem. First, it is generally difficult to find MDs who are interested in pursuing academic research. The Worcester area has also suffered by being tantalizingly close, but not close enough, to Boston. By making it clear that the company is seeking outspoken and creative individuals, rather than simply technically expert individuals, Chick and Hayes have been successful in their recruiting efforts. But in the long run, the Center of Excellence will make the area more attractive by creating a large community of professionals.

Funding problems were solved by realizing that typical venture capitalists would resist investing in a company with such an unavoidably long development stage. Funding came instead through a joint-venture agreement with a large corporate sponsor which recently acquired the biomedical research firm from which Chick has purchased membranes and other tissues for over five years. The agreement provides Biohybrid with research contracts, which combined with supporting research projects, would amount to a $50 million total investment by the time the project reaches commercialization. Profits are not expected for seven years. But here, too, Chick's relationship with the Center of Excellence at the UMass Medical School has been helpful. The medical school conducts the surgery on the animals in which the implant devices are to be tested, thus leveraging Biohybrid resources while contributing to basic research.

Dr. Chick has been successful at amassing the resources he has needed to get Biohybrid under way—but imagine how many more lives could have been saved had he been able to get these relationships going sooner. Now, the Center of Excellence is there to facilitate the growth of Biohybrid.

Extending Innovation to Mature Industries

An emphasis on tomorrow's technologies cannot come at the expense of today's jobs—and that often means established firms in mature industries. In 1983, the first year of my second term, over 12,000 people in Massachusetts saw their jobs disappear as sixty-seven facilities across the state closed their doors. The greatest number of closings came from mature industries: manufacturers of apparel, shoes, and electrical machinery.

Our most pressing concern was an obvious one: how to deal with the effects of economic dislocation when plants were closed or jobs became obsolete. The other concern was preventative: how to help mature industries modernize and remain competitive so that jobs were saved and even expanded. This second concern fit squarely within our strategy of investing in innovation.

With the help of business, labor, and academic advisers, we developed two important ideas for revitalizing mature industries through technological innovation. One involved the *development of new products*, the other the *application of new processes*.

INNOVATION IN PRODUCT DEVELOPMENT

The Commission on the Future of Mature Industries was formed in June 1983 to help think through some tough and controversial issues with regard both to plant closings and to revitalizing mature companies. One of its recommendations was the creation of a Massachusetts Product Development Corporation—modeled after the Massachusetts Technology Development Corporation but designed for mature firms bringing new products to market.

The Massachusetts Product Development Corporation (MPDC) was established by the legislature and is now under way. It provides initial funding, typically between $50,000 and $200,000, for new-product ideas that are technologically innovative and of demonstrated practicality. Although there is no formal requirement, funded organizations are likely to be in manufacturing.

MPDC serves as a funder of last resort, providing its stake in exchange for royalties and thus not burdening the company with debt. This enables the company to obtain more conventional sources of funds, using as collateral the still untouched asset base of the company.

By mid-1987, three products had been funded. The first is made by Microtool, a small Ashby firm that was recently sold by its founding family to an entrepreneur with an interest in its growth. The new product is a microprocessor-based weighing system which improves on a device developed in Iceland and manufactured and distributed by Microtool under license. This new Micro Weighing System allows packages of, say, machine parts or vegetables to be assembled precisely to a final specified weight. Now such packages are systematically overfilled to ensure that the weight specified is a minimum; since the overage can be considerable, so can savings. The $150,000 from MPDC was matched with a similar amount from both Microtool and a venture capitalist, and marketing efforts are now under way. If successful, the product will result in fifty new jobs.

A second new product, produced by a company in Southeastern Massachusetts, is an innovative means of blowing surplus water and waste from raw-paper-mill feed. Traditionally, this has been done by suction, a process that is both energy-intensive and difficult to control. This new process is of such interest that the Boxboard Manufacturers Association has itself agreed to invest in it.

The third MPDC investment represents an extension of what has been up to now a sideline for the only American wigmaker, located in rural Massachusetts. Its technology permits effective production of specialty wigs and even whole pelts, used by such wig consumers as the Muppets and Walt Disney. MPDC funds will enable the company to retool for a major emphasis on these products.

INNOVATION ON THE SHOP FLOOR

In the fall of 1985 I led tours of leaders from the private and public sectors to every region of the state, visiting forty-five companies and meeting with several hundred local citizens in each area. In January 1986, I convened a State House Conference on Innovation and empaneled the Governor's Advisory Council on Innovation.

The council recommended the creation of a sixth Center of Excellence focused on applied technology and productivity. Unlike the other centers, which focused on developing new products for the marketplace, the applied technology center would help Massachusetts industries make traditional products in new, more competitive ways. Manufacturing experts, such as Harvard Business School's Robert Hayes, believe that such *process* innovations—becoming better at the manufacturing—are as important as *product* innovations in keeping American industry competitive. I agree with him.

The new center is just getting underway. It will be a network of industrial greenhouses, where engineers can develop new production technologies—many of them computer-driven and highly automated—and tailor them for the shop floors of Massachusetts industry. It will promote a new and stronger relationship among schools of engineering, mature manufacturing companies, and the leading makers of new process technologies, including Massachusetts companies like Automated Assemblies in Clinton, Automatix in Bedford, and Aeonics in Billerica. Academic centers at Worcester Polytech and the University of Lowell will make important contributions.

In addition to its role in fostering process innovations, the applied technology center will help companies deal with the very real human issues that change brings to established firms, issues ranging from retraining and retooling to cooperation between management and unions in getting ready for change. The center will be a place where management and labor can come together to exchange ideas and plan the modernization of the state's mature industries.

CHAPTER THREE

Streets, Parks, and Houses: Rebuilding the Fabric

Economic growth may be measured in numbers, but it happens in places. And while government's role in individual business decisions is secondary, its role in making communities large and small into suitable hosts for private investment is primary and indispensable.

In a United States Commerce Department survey of two thousand top American firms, over half said that their first priority in choosing a site for expansion was a solid public infrastructure of roads, water, and utilities. In Massachusetts, we have understood for over a decade that the economic infrastructure of a community includes much more than those important nuts and bolts. It also includes how the community looks and feels, whether it is rebuilding or declining, whether it has a sense of itself that embraces its heritage and its future—or not.

We were not interested in paving everything over or developing everywhere. In Massachusetts, the natural and built environments of places large and small are essential not only to the quality of life, but to the calculus of those who make business decisions. So we set out to create *and* preserve. Alongside new public and private construction, we began to restore what could still be used, turning vacant mills into housing and schools and offices and industrial incubators. We tried to smooth the way for enterprises to operate and grow and for people to find affordable housing and get to work. We were as determined to preserve some kinds of land as we were to build on others. We worked on short-term programs that would nurture opportunity and innovation now, and on long-term initiatives that would anticipate the needs of the year 2000 and beyond.

We started in Lowell, where the Commonwealth joined hands with then Congressman Paul Tsongas and a host of community leaders to rebuild the fabric of a great city on the edge of economic ruin.

The Comeback City of the Comeback State

In 1975, Massachusetts was the symbol of everything that had gone wrong with urban America, and Lowell was the symbol of everything that had gone wrong in Massachusetts.

Annual unemployment was hovering near 16 percent. The once-elegant downtown was a picture of decay. The textile mills had long since left, with nothing visible to take their place. People were talking about knocking down the mills and filling in the canals. Students coming out of Lowell High School had one thought—to get far away from Lowell and never come back. There was no new investment, no new jobs, and not much hope.

Who would have believed then that in just a decade half a million people a year would visit Lowell, or that unemployment in that city would shrink to 4 percent, or that there would be more construction per capita in Lowell than in Houston, Los Angeles, or Miami?

By 1987, the comeback had produced 42,000 new jobs in greater Lowell, and more are being created every year. Downtown Lowell has become a national model for successful revitalization, not as a museum piece but as a vital center of commerce. The location of Wang Laboratories' world headquarters in Lowell has made it a prestigious business address, bringing other companies to the area. The neighborhoods adjoining the downtown are starting to come back, and the entire Merrimack Valley—named after the historic river of commerce flowing through Lowell—is starting to blossom.

"Lowell weaves a spell," proclaimed a 1985 article in the *National Geographic Traveler*. Oases of open space surround canals and the Merrimack River. A Lowell walking tour points to an astonishing seventy-five historic buildings with a rich array of architectural forms. Many of them, like the Old Worthen Tavern, were built in the 1820s. Canal boat tours show off the locks and a classic Lowell mill. A waterpower exhibit has a working antique loom. But even more impressive is the fact that most of the historic buildings are back at work—as factories, offices, schools, condominiums, and housing for the elderly.

Every piece of the Massachusetts economic strategy played a role in the Lowell revival. But most of all, the Lowell story demonstrates the importance of public infrastructure for economic development. Lowell involved rebuilding in the literal sense, brick by brick, building by building. And every row of bricks rebuilt some of the human spirit of the place, too.

Lowell took its name from Francis Cabot Lowell, the first entrepreneur to tap the waterpower of the Merrimack River when he built a textile mill along its banks in 1821. The growth of the textile industry transformed Lowell from a sparsely populated rural area into the state's second largest city. By 1900 Massachusetts was the world's largest producer of woven fabrics, much of it made in Lowell. By the early 1920s, employment in the textile mills accounted for over 40 percent of all manufacturing employment in Lowell. But then Lowell's dramatic growth halted abruptly. Manufacturing employment fell by almost half between 1924 and 1932, and that was only partially due to the Great Depression. Much of New England's textile industry shifted to the South during this period (and later to Asia). When the national economy recovered, Lowell did not.

KEYS TO THE CITY: HOW LOWELL WAS RESTORED

In 1975 an act of the Massachusetts legislature established the Lowell Development and Financial Corporation, a consortium of local bankers which could offer low-cost loans for historically appropriate renovations. Its first president, George Duncan, now head of the First Bank of Lowell, had been inspired by the Riverwalk area along the canals in downtown San Antonio, Texas, as a possible model for renewing Lowell's own riverfront and canals. Other community leaders also had dreams for Lowell. Model cities Director Patrick Mogan thought about using downtown Lowell as a classroom, as a vehicle for learning about America's industrial history. Paul Tsongas, whose public career had begun on the Lowell City Council, signed on and became the champion of the project.

As a candidate and then as a brand-new governor, I listened to these dreams and was touched by them. The Dukakis family was no stranger to Lowell, for this wonderful old city was the gateway through which my father had passed on his way from young Greek immigrant to Massachusetts physician. In 1975 I named Frank Keefe, Lowell's young city planning director, as the first head of my Development Cabinet, and told my people to get to work. The first project seemed simple enough, but it was extraordinarily difficult. Since the very buildings of Lowell that now seemed too run-down to use were an important part of American industrial history, why not turn them into a living museum? Yet Massachusetts had no program for rebuilding its cities, let alone through historic parks. Innovation was required at every step of the way. The $10 million that Massachusetts committed to the Lowell Urban Heritage State Park in 1975 was followed by $40 million which Congress secured for the Lowell National Urban Park. Today the two park systems are thoroughly interwoven, providing attractive amenities for tourists, residents, workers, and shoppers. They are a magnet for cultural, theatrical, and educational activities. Turning a stagnating city into America's great urban park was like making the desert bloom.

Another turning point was the 1976 decision by Dr. An Wang to move the headquarters of Wang Laboratories from Tewksbury, a nearby small town, to Lowell by 1978. Wang is an almost unparalleled example of entrepreneurial success. In 1976 this computer manufacturer had revenues of not quite $100 million; by June 1987 worldwide revenues were about $3 billion. When the company outgrew its space in Tewksbury and was looking for a new site, Dr. Wang was attracted by a building in Lowell designed for CBS Electronics in the 1950s by a well-known Japanese architect and subsequently owned by Avco and Mostek. The building came with sixteen acres at a reasonable price.

> At the time I looked at the property, [Lowell] was a somewhat down-at-the-heels city that had been declining since its heyday. It had often been cited as an example of the failure of the industrial cities of the Northeast to adapt to changes in the world economy. It was also a highly unionized city, with a government whose leaders squabbled among themselves while businesses and young people left in droves . . . Indeed, it hardly seemed an auspicious place to move one's headquarters. But this is what we did. [An Wang with Eugene Linden, *Lessons: An Autobiography*, Addison Wesley, 1986]

Today, the three towers of Wang's corporate headquarters tell the world that Lowell, Massachusetts—the premier American industrial city of the nineteenth century—will play an important role in the twenty-first.

A third factor was the development of grass-roots community

planning. In 1979 the Lowell Plan, Inc., was founded—a non-profit private development corporation billed as a partnership for economic development with a vision that "goes beyond the ordinary." In concert with city and state government, its long-range goal was to "make Lowell the best, most livable mid-size city in America." By 1986 there were 117 members, running the gamut from small proprietorships such as the Henry Achin Insurance Agency and Brian Pest Control to giants such as Raytheon and Wang. Through 1986, $2.6 million had been raised from private donations to implement a five-point strategy: office, industrial, and retail development; parking and access; housing development; canalway enhancement; and quality of life.

Among other achievements, the Lowell Plan was a major factor in getting a new Hilton hotel to Lowell, a facility that would further build tourist and commercial business. Arthur Robbins, developer of the Lowell Hilton, said:

> There is not a doubt in my mind. Without the Lowell Plan, there would not have been a hotel. The Lowell Plan purchased property for the project, acted as facilitator, and championed the project throughout. It is also gratifying to belong to an organization with a dynamic vision for economic development that benefits the entire community . . . I've never seen anything like the cooperation between public and private sector that you've got in this city.

The city agreed to upgrade road access to the hotel, got federal funds for parking, and negotiated with Wang Laboratories to put a new world training facility next door. In the same part of the downtown, the state funded two major parking garages, an expansion of the heritage park, renovation of the Lowell Civic Auditorium, and a long-awaited scenic boulevard from the nearby superhighway into the heart of the city.

Restoring Lowell involved more than bricks and mortar, of course, but even educational institutions reside in buildings. When other cities were demolishing their downtown high schools, Lowell and the Commonwealth collaborated to renovate and expand old Lowell High, in the heart of the Heritage Park district. And then there's the University of Lowell.

In 1975, Lowell State College and Lowell Technical Institute were merged to form ULowell. Since that time, the university has built a national reputation and attracted a strong student body by clearly defining its goals: its primary mission is research and teaching in applied science and technology. The university specializes in engineering, computer science, and management. It ranks with MIT as one of the top five colleges nationwide in providing technical employees for the state's high-tech firms. But while MIT's tuition is around $12,000 a year, tuition at ULowell is less than $1,600 for Massachusetts residents.

Over the next decade, the commonwealth will invest some $300 million in the University of Lowell, an ambitious expansion plan designed to make ULowell into the economic engine for the Merrimack Valley. Franklyn Jenifer, chancellor of the Massachusetts Board of Regents, says, "Lowell is out front. It is poised for national excellence."

Most of the ULowell building expansion will occur in the old Lawrence Mills, less than a mile from the ULowell north campus. The mills will be renovated into laboratories and classroom space; there will also be incubator space for the start-up companies which the university research is expected to spawn. A new in-town campus for Middlesex Community College will be built as a companion project, and the two schools will work together closely.

At the moment, the Merrimack Valley is the most underserved area for higher education in Massachusetts. The expansion of ULowell clearly indicates our determination to provide full access to institutions of higher learning and strong technical support to new and old businesses in the area. The investment will pay off. A study by economist and ULowell Business School dean Benjamin Chinitz projected that by the end of this century, the university will be pumping $420 million per year into the regional economy.

GOOD JOBS IN DIVERSE BUSINESSES: FROM SOFTWARE TO SPAGHETTI

Lowell today has a good business mix. The highly visible Wang Laboratories world headquarters, now joined by such nearby companies as Apollo Computer, Valiant Technologies, and a clutch of small software and computer firms in the historic Wannalancit Mills, may make it seem as if Lowell's success rests solely on the high-tech boom. But many other innovative companies, in other industries, have flourished as the city has flourished. None is more important than the Prince Company. What could be less "high tech" than pasta?

The Prince Macaroni Company was established in 1912, when three Italian immigrants incorporated their small pasta company and named it after its location on Prince Street in the Italian North End of Boston. Prince moved to Lowell in the 1930s and has since grown to become the largest U.S. manufacturer of pasta products. In 1987 it was bought by Borden for $164 million.

From its New England base, where it holds over 50 percent of the pasta market with its Prince line (and over 75 percent if one includes the private-label products it produces), Prince now sells its regular pasta, including over fifty different cuts, in many other regions. In Chicago, it is the number one brand, in Michigan, it is number two, and in New York, it is number four.

Prince was an innovator in production processes, in marketing, and in the products themselves. Seven years ago it began a $40 million asset-improvement program which brought new technology into the production facility, led by its engineering division. Recently the marketing group developed a creative mail-order catalog of pasta products and related gift items. Prince is also a product leader. As President Joseph Pellegrino put it, "We've always innovated with more daring." New products included Superoni, a high-protein pasta; Light, a reduced-calorie pasta; and pasta flavored with basil and other spices.

When Prince was concerned about a traffic problem affecting its trucks and thought about moving, Lowell responded by agreeing to build a twelve-hundred-foot access road to the manufacturing plant. To continue its expansion, in 1984 Prince acquired a 50 percent stake in the New England Milling Company in Ayer, Massachusetts, which processes wheat into flour. The state helped with an industrial revenue bond from the Massachusetts Industrial Finance Agency (MIFA).

Lowell now attracts between ten and fifteen private dollars for every public dollar invested. Lowell's success has become a nationwide model for revitalization for old industrial cities. A dozen years ago, when we were first working on the Lowell project, we did not really know if it would succeed and bear fruit. It has, and that experience made the work that followed that much easier.

Following Lowell's Lead: Springfield and Fitchburg

The mid-seventies were not good times for Springfield either. For three centuries the economic and governmental capital of the Connecticut Valley, this proud old city had embarked on an ambitious but conventional program of urban renewal, with mixed results. Some important downtown developments had occurred—among them, a civic center and an in-town commercial complex—but the limitations of the urban renewal approach were plain. Gaping holes still pocked Main Street, where "renewal" had brought demolition but no redevelopment. There was little relationship between new construction and the wealth of historic buildings and cultural resources still available in the downtown. Whatever economic benefits renewal brought were not yet being felt in the neighborhoods, the city as a whole, or the surrounding region. In 1975 unemployment was 12.9 percent in Springfield, and 11.3 percent in Greater Springfield.

The community answered the challenge, forging a partnership between City Hall and a nonprofit leadership group, Springfield Central, Inc. They created a thoughtful, visionary, and caring master plan for the rebirth of downtown Springfield. They began a decade-long mastery of Urban Development Action Grants and other federal revitalization programs that became a national model of how those initiatives were meant to be used.

But equally important, they turned to Commonwealth and found an eager and committed partner. In 1988, our portfolio of state investments in downtown Springfield includes:

- A heritage state park which has restored Court Square to its historic role as a center of cultural and social life for the region.
- The new Basketball Hall of Fame, a national tourist destination and a catalyst for a sweeping revitalization of the riverfront that is now being planned
- A Western State House, a parking garage, and a key state welfare office in the old Paramount Theater—three state investments which anchor the revitalization of the North Blocks district
- MIFA financing for fourteen new construction and historic rehabilitation projects, representing $52 million in private investment
- Columbus Center, an attractive downtown garage wrapped around a theater which has brought regional stage productions back to Springfield
- State funds of $5.6 million to help bring about the $118 million Monarch Place commercial and hotel project—the largest commercial real-estate development outside of Boston ever undertaken in Massachusetts. With Monarch, the rebirth of downtown Springfield has come full circle, for it was the closing of the landmark Forbes & Wallace de-

partment store on this same site in 1976 that sparked this community's public-private partnership for economic revitalization

Downtown Springfield, like downtown Lowell, is now a national success story. It has helped drop the unemployment rate in Greater Springfield to 2.3 percent. Like downtown Lowell, it is the nerve center of a valleywide reinvestment in industry and technology. And we are helping both cities translate downtown success into breakthroughs in housing and the quality of life in nearby neighborhoods.

Sometimes what appears to be a simple improvement can have far-reaching effects. A new parking garage in Fitchburg played a role in keeping that city's General Electric plant alive and well. As an old mill town, Fitchburg's roads were not laid out to accommodate cars, especially not *parked* cars. Since the mid-1970s Fitchburg's central business district had been in decline, largely because of regional malls which offer shoppers the advantage of on-site parking lots. A planning committee, formed to assess the future of downtown Fitchburg, determined that lack of parking was the most serious problem.

The city built its first parking garage in 1980, and it has been managed since by PRIDE, a home-grown non-profit organization. The garage was so successful in luring shoppers that additional parking was needed. In 1983 planning began for a second garage, and the city turned to the State House for assistance. Fitchburg obtained $2.8 million—70 percent of the needed funds—from our Off-Street Parking Program. The remaining 30 percent came from several sources: a $500,000 federal Community Development Block Grant was issued to the city; the city donated the land, valued at $200,000. Lastly, PRIDE, the management company, agreed to put up $700,000. The banks that supported PRIDE's portion of the deal, however, insisted on firm evidence that its money would be well-invested.

That commitment came from General Electric's downtown

Fitchburg facility. GE guaranteed 50 percent usage of the garage, and paid a fee in advance to cover the rental of those spaces. The deal made good sense to GE—it had been acutely affected by the city's lack of parking. The issue had for years been a headache for GE employees and a source of tension between the company and the city. The GE steam turbine and compressor plant is Fitchburg's largest employer, and the eight-hundred-job downtown plant is a key to the city's revitalization efforts. One GE manager noted that his company's role in building the garage was "a good investment. We solved a problem that was a real pain for our employees, and we've made a contribution to the city."

While parking might seem like a trivial issue for a giant company such as GE, it was related to a fundamental problem faced by the plant. As part of a multinational corporation under pressure to cut costs and increase competitiveness, the Fitchburg operation is in a touch-and-go business—heavy manufacturing. Though GE's plants in other parts of the state have undergone large layoffs due to companywide reductions in the transformer and turbine divisions, Fitchburg has recently reorganized its management structure, reoriented its product line, and modernized its production process. The company has invested nearly $40 million in new equipment and process lines—in part because of assistance with that sticky parking problem.

The Acid Test: Urban Neighborhoods

In many ways, the acid test of our commitment to rebuild the economic fabric of Massachusetts is Boston's Southwest Corridor and Blue Hill Avenue, where most of the city's black and Hispanic citizens live. Here in the shadow of America's hottest downtown economy is a community devastated by decades of high unemployment and massive disinvestment. Mayor Ray Flynn and I were not about to give up on these neighborhoods.

In 1983 I created the Governor's Community Development Co-ordinating Council, a leadership group of neighborhood residents and entrepreneurs, legislators, and city officials through which the community helps shape each of the principal state investments. Our goal was not merely to employ people or to complete projects. It was to create the full measure of opportunity that comes with a strong and growing neighborhhood economy.

In May of 1987, after a decade of construction, we opened the $743 million Southwest Corridor project—to date the largest public infrastructure project in the history of New England. It involved the relocation of a rapid transit line, AMTRAK, and our southwest commuter rail system—not only an investment in better transportation but a watershed investment in the economic future of a half-dozen Boston neighborhoods. Eighty-five acres of new parkland line the corridor's length. A decade ago, in anticipation of the project's completion, the Commonwealth helped bring new mixed-income housing and a Digital Equipment Company assembly plant to Roxbury and made a commitment to a new campus for Roxbury Community College. In 1985 we secured full funding for the college and broke ground. The $40 million Southwest Corridor campus admitted its first students this winter, fulfilling a ten-year-old dream.

Under Mayor Flynn, the city of Boston has joined the Commonwealth and the community in a strong partnership to bring genuine opportunity to the people who live and work along the corridor—through thousands of new commercial and industrial jobs, hundreds of new units of housing, equity participation by minority businesses and developers, and badly needed training for area residents.

In a single dramatic project—the creation of a major, mixed-use complex at what is known as Parcel 18—the state and city intend to bring four thousand jobs to the corridor. In joining Mayor Flynn's parcel-to-parcel linkage program, we have coupled our development initiative at Parcel 18 with the city's disposition of a prime downtown development site near

Chinatown. The combined development rights are worth up to $400 million, and a local team of Black, Hispanic, and Asian developers will hold a major share of the equity. In addition, at least 30 percent of the development services must be performed by minority businesses. Together, we will forge a new set of relationships between metropolitan Boston's growing service economy and the area's minority builders, lawyers, architects, bankers, accountants, and developers.

Four miles south of Parcel 18, we are planning a second anchor project at the Dorchester campus of Boston State Hospital. There the state is preparing to offer a large tract of surplus land —one of the largest new development sites in the recent history of metropolitan Boston—for a mix of office, industrial, and residential development.

Two of the neighborhood's principal business districts, Dudley Station and Grove Hall, are each the focus of a comprehensive revitalization strategy in which state investments play a key role. At Dudley, the traditional "downtown" of Roxbury, a heritage state park and the reuse of the historic station terminal as a transit and retail center will set the stage for sustained private investment.

The Massachusetts Housing Partnership

Decent and affordable housing is an indispensable part of the American dream and of Massachusetts' economic fabric.

In 1985 we created the Massachusetts Housing Partnership, a distinguished board of forty public and private members providing overall policy guidance and expertise to the Commonwealth. The partnership has quickly become an institution.

Far more than a single program or even an overall policy, the partnership is a full-scale mobilization of economic resources and political will. The partnership is not only a *statewide* alliance, important as that is. It is a family of *local* alliances for decent, affordable housing.

Some one hundred and twenty cities and towns have already secured designations as "Massachusetts Housing Partnership Communities"—recognition that a solid and creative housing agenda is in place and that the full array of state housing resources will be brought to bear. Mayor Flynn and I announced Boston's designation in 1986, and with it a $71 million state commitment for affordable housing.

Affordable housing in Massachusetts means three things: public housing, mixed-income rental housing, and affordable home ownership. In the face of the virtual abandonment by Washington of a national commitment to affordable housing in America, all three of these present formidable challenges. We intend to meet them.

Less than half a dozen states have their own public housing programs. But in Massachusetts we have pioneered the development of low-density public housing designed to fit in with its surrounding neighborhoods. And we have made livable, safe, and attractive public housing part of our basic commitment to provide housing opportunity for all Massachusetts citizens.

In 1983, 1985, and 1987, the Legislature enacted the three largest public housing bond issues in the history of the Commonwealth, representing thousands of new and renovated units. The results thus far are dramatic. More than 150 Massachusetts cities and towns are now developing new public housing for families, including many suburban and rural communities.

In 1983 Massachusetts created the nation's first state loan program to support the development of mixed-income rental housing. Administered by the Massachusetts Housing Finance Agency, the new program—State Housing Assistance for Rental Production, or SHARP—reduces the permanent mortgage interest rate for the developer to as little as 5 percent and requires in exchange that at least 25 percent of the units be available to low-income households. So far SHARP has made the difference in financing sixty-six projects, now occupied or under development, providing nearly eight thousand units of housing. In older city, town, and neighborhood centers, SHARP has meant the restoration of key buildings or renewal parcels that had long frustrated community revitalization efforts. In the suburbs, SHARP has helped make mixed-income housing a welcome addition to several communities.

Thanks to the Commonwealth's strong economy, the number of families and individuals who are ready to purchase their first homes greatly exceeds the affordable supply. Traditional low-interest mortgage programs, which have helped tens of thousands in Massachusetts buy their first homes, do not encourage new housing production and are no longer sufficient to close the pricing gap between supply and demand.

In January 1986, we announced a homeownership opportunity program to give thousands of moderate-income households their first chance to buy and own a house. This new program combined low-interest mortgage financing, a new fund to reduce interest rates, and grants to cities and towns for the cost of new roads, sidewalks, and sewers to support affordable housing development. The result of this initiative is mortgage rates as low as 5 percent for first-time buyers and strong incentives for local government to work with private developers to produce new, mixed-income housing.

The homeownership opportunity program has become an immediate success. In just over two years, ninety-six new homeownership developments have begun design or construction all across Massachusetts, representing nearly 6,000 units. Many families have had the opportunity to buy a house, in developments from Fitchburg's Cleghorn neighborhood to Dorchester's Champlain Circle. Young families can buy decent housing for $60,000 to $110,000 at interest rates they can afford. Our goal for the next five years is an ambitious one: 15,000 new homes for first-time buyers.

As many as 5,000 private housing units in Massachusetts are abandoned, and uncounted house lots are vacant. These properties stand witness to the twin frustrations of neighborhood disinvestment and lack of affordable housing. In 1984, legislation was enacted easing the transfer of vacant, tax-titled property from local governments to willing developers, and began the process of targeting our production resources toward the reclamation of abandoned properties. We intend, over the next five years, to reclaim them all.

Much of this state's abandoned housing is in Boston, and through the Boston Housing Partnership, the city is beginning to turn those properties around. But other Massachusetts cities also offer dramatic examples of what we can accomplish together.

Barely five blocks from the resurgent center of Lowell is a neighborhood known as The Acre—for three generations the home of Lowell's immigrant poor. Today the Acre is home to the city's Hispanic and Asian minorities, and the overall lack of opportunity is reflected most plainly in the erosion of The Acre's housing stock. But that is changing.

Through a partnership of the city, several state agencies, and a community development corporation called The Coalition for a Better Acre, a combination of rental and ownership production is reclaiming abandoned buildings and lots, providing affordable dwellings, and rekindling hope for the community's future.

Finally, many Massachusetts communities have let growth and development get ahead of their ability to manage it. Communities are particularly concerned when scarce land resources are consumed by large-scale residential construction that their own people cannot afford. More often than not, the choices appear to be either allowing unrestricted growth or enacting a sudden moratorium. Neither is a good choice for most communities.

As part of the Massachusetts Housing Partnership, we are helping communities examine their housing needs—developing affordable housing solutions that also respect their land-use, conservation, and economic development needs. In the Connecticut Valley and the Blackstone Valley, on the Cape and the South Shore, we are looking to creative local officials and citizens to provide answers that we can use all over the state. Many communities are already changing their zoning to make clustered homes and open-space preservation a reality.

This need to balance housing development and open space preservation brings us to a broader issue—how we think about growth, change, and community character as we rebuild the fabric of our state.

City and Town Centers: A Growth Philosophy

As the Lowell experiment was getting under way, so was a much broader effort to plan for the revival of Massachusetts communities. In 1975, we asked our cities and towns to take some time and think about their futures. How much growth did they want, and where? What did they think it would take to make their wishes a reality?

The 1977 Massachusetts Growth Policy Report, *City and Town Centers: A Program for Growth*, demonstrated that communities of all sizes saw their economic future, their sense of self, and their place in the fabric of the Commonwealth bound up in the well-being of their centers—from large downtowns to neighborhood business districts to village centers. Eleven years later, we are still following many of the steps that individual communities laid out in 1977.

For the cities and towns, a healthy downtown means a better chance for private investment throughout the area. For the state, city and town centers represent an opportunity to invest our infrastructure dollars efficiently, by rebuilding and improving existing streets, parks, sewer systems, and public buildings. And many of the people most in need of new economic opportunity—minorities, the elderly, young families, small business-men—live or work in established city, town, and neighborhood centers.

For decades before 1975, Massachusetts, like many industrial states, had badly neglected its city and town centers. Yet it was clear that if private investment was to save our communities from unemployment and decay, the Commonwealth would first have to join with local governments to lay the foundation.

Heritage parks were the first step. The program was, in a real sense, the opposite of urban renewal; rather than tearing down a city's past, we sought to recapture the riverfronts, streetscapes, and industrial heritage that make our city centers special. In 1978, once the Lowell Urban Heritage State Park was under way, we designated seven more regional cities as sites for heritage parks. Those parks have helped create exciting mixed-use developments—from the waterfronts of Fall River and Lynn to Springfield's ancient Court Square to the once-derelict "Western Gateway" rail yards of North Adams.

These heritage parks have become important instruments of change. "Before the heritage park, our downtown was a waste-land," said Carlton Viveiros, since 1977 the mayor of Fall River. After the park's completion in 1983, it became a focal point for downtown revitalization and created a tie to a nearby Portu-guese neighborhood. Since 1983, we have begun work on five more heritage parks and helped some two dozen small towns revive their historic greens and commons.

A second key investment strategy for city and town centers was the Commercial Area Revitalization District (CARD) pro-gram. Interest rates were a serious barrier to private redevelop-ment efforts in older urban centers. If money for pioneering downtown real-estate projects cost the same as for conventional suburban developments, investment dollars would flow to the latter. Industrial revenue bonds (IRBs) offered an established method of lowering interest rates on long-term debt, but their use in Massachusetts, as in most states, was restricted to indus-trial projects. Some states did allow IRBs to be used for commercial development, but without any geographic restriction, so that IRBs were more likely to compete with downtown revitalization than to assist it.

In 1978, Massachusetts made commercial projects eligible for IRB financing, but only in established city and town centers designated as CARDs. In the next nine years, over $600 million of private commercial development in downtown and neighborhood business districts have been financed through IRBs. Scarcely a downtown in Massachusetts has failed to use this unique financing tool to launch the reinvestment of private capital in new construction, the reuse of historic buildings, and the creation of new jobs in the heart of town. Although federal tax reform recently ended the use of IRBs for commercial projects, CARD projects will continue to be a state priority for taxable bonds and other creative financing techniques.

Third, we recognized the attractive marriage that could be made between historic buildings looking for a new use and affordable housing opportunities looking for a place to happen. In 1978, we began awarding state housing funds to communities that would use them in strategic downtown locations. In 1988, our new program for rental housing production—the SHARP mortgage reduction loan—is being used to revitalize landmark downtown buildings like Gardner's Heywood-Wakefield Mill, Leominster's Whitney Carriage Factory, and Clinton's Philbin Block.

Fourth, we recognized the value of locating major state government activities downtown. A commitment that began with the decision in 1976 to build a new Registry of Motor Vehicles in downtown Worcester rather than six miles out of town has matured in 1988 into the Western State House in downtown Springfield, a campus of North Shore Community College in the heart of Lynn's downtown revitalization district, and a conscious policy of placing welfare, revenue, and employment offices in downtown buildings whenever possible.

A fifth initiative was the Massachusetts Government Land Bank. The Land Bank, created in 1975 during my first administration to manage the conversion of closed military bases to civilian use, has evolved into an agency that helps cities and towns with a broader range of development opportunities. By providing creative financing to private enterprise or public agencies in the development of commercial, industrial, and residential projects, the Land Bank works to revitalize older communities, increase the availablity of low- and moderate-income housing, provide jobs, expand the local tax base, and leverage additional public and private investment. Land Bank projects range from the Lechmere Canal high-tech center in East Cambridge to conversion of Dorchester's landmark Baker Chocolate Mill to mixed income housing, from development of Gloucester's Inner Harbor as a fish-processing center to the redevelopment of the Old Library in Lawrence as professional office space.

Massachusetts continues to invest in older commercial districts more fully and flexibly than any other state:

- We provide Community Development Action Grants for a variety of local development projects—if communities can line up commitments for private investment. Funds are used for sidewalks, roads, waterfront and park reconstruction, sewer lines, and railway spurs. The CDAG program has created or retained over 20,000 jobs and leveraged some $200 million of private investment.
- We help our cities absorb what is often the most costly and the most critical downtown infrastructure need—off-street parking. Since 1983, our unique program of 70 percent state grant assistance for parking facilities in CARD districts has resulted in dozens of facilities in downtowns across Massachusetts.
- We share with our historic regional cities the cost of civic and cultural centers—from a major commitment to the convention centers of Boston and Worcester, to New Bedford's Zeiterion Theatre and Holyoke's Children's Museum.

The other side of investing in city and town centers is to preserve what is special in Massachusetts. The two principles are not mutually exclusive—the whole theory of heritage parks is that in this historic Commonwealth, preservation and development are compatible and sometimes identical.

Often, however, the state and its communities must simply decide that some places should not be developed. Parkland, farmland, and wetlands are at the heart of this state's quality of life, and we need to protect them.

We must also protect our rivers, ponds, and aquifers from contamination and unnecessary depletion. It costs a lot less to keep development out of a watershed than it does to clean up a drinking water supply that has been poisoned.

We must reassert the fundamental link between our coastline and all other aspects of our economic life. We must encourage those activities that depend on our place by the sea, while protecting the fragile ecology of the coastline's undeveloped areas.

We are doing all of these things through a combination of tough land-use regulations and a program of public investment in land preservation that is unmatched anywhere in America. In 1984, the legislature approved a $162 million bond issue for open space and public parks. In 1987, we topped that with a bond issue of half a billion dollars.

The fruits of this public investment can be seen in every kind of setting and in virtually every Massachusetts community. Alongside our investment in historic downtowns is a sweeping expansion and improvement of what is already the sixth-largest state park system in America. Tens of millions of dollars have been dedicated to acquiring aquifer and watershed lands, river and stream corridors, and swatches of our precious coastline that deserve to remain undeveloped and open to our people.

I'm especially proud of what we've done to save Massachusetts agriculture. In the summer of 1987 Boston's venerable Faneuil Hall was the setting for the annual Massachusetts tomato festival. My agriculture commissioner, August Schumacher, enticed veteran reporter Neal Pierce to serve as a judge. Pierce wrote in the August 23, 1987, *Boston Globe*:

What business, you ask, did a grass-roots government columnist have among food editors, supermarket execs, and certified farmer judges? . . . But if you think problem solving is government's job, Massachusetts' farm policy is worth a look. [*Boston Globe*, 8/23/87]

In my first administration we saw farmland being engulfed by subdivisions, shopping centers, and industrial parks, so we created a $25 million bond fund to buy agricultural development rights; so far this program has saved more than 21,000 acres and 200 farms. The next step was to help local farmers find markets. We launched a television campaign, pushed city farmers' markets, invited supermarket managers to monthly meetings to discuss the virtues of home-grown products, and gave 14,000 poor women and children $10 food coupons redeemable for fresh Massachusetts-grown produce at the farmers' markets—putting cash in farmers' pockets while promoting healthier diets for the disadvantaged.

The success of these efforts, and their adoption by other states, has encouraged us to further support the preservation of farmland for farming in environmentally responsible ways. About $200 million in MIFA loans have gone to form or expand food-processing firms. A state "integrated pest management" program has cut back sharply on chemicals used on food crops. State subsidies support composting machines to reduce the need for chemical fertilizers and landfills. And that massive 1987 open-space bond issue includes $35 million more for our agricultural development rights purchase fund.

Is there economic value in this strong preservationist ethic? In a Harvard Business School study of thirty innovative companies throughout the state, respondents were asked to rate seventeen factors that could be advantages or disadvantages in their part of the state. "Quality of life" was ranked number one as an advantage, even ahead of "brainpower" and "technical information." In evaluating the benefits of being in Massachusetts, 43 percent of the companies mentioned proximity to the academic community, but 33 percent also mentioned "physical setting" and "quality of life."

Another study of 117 Massachusetts high-tech firms found that many executives supported environmental laws because they improve the quality of life. A medical-equipment manufacturer declared, "I don't want to go boating on the river and have the bottom fall out of the boat." [Mark Templer, "Entrepreneurial High Technology Economic Development in Massachusetts," unpublished Masters thesis for MIT Sloan School, 1984]

CHAPTER FOUR

Training and Education for Tomorrow's Work Force: Investments in People

A training and education system that ensures the development of our *human* resources is critical to a strong and vibrant economic future. American productivity and innovation rest on the skills and talents of our people. Developing and improving those skills and talents are a fundamental responsibility of government and one of the best investments we can make.

When my second administration began in 1983, Massachusetts stood at a critical juncture. A changing, more knowledge-intensive economy was creating an unprecedented demand for qualified labor and a growing awareness of the importance of a work force well educated in the basics and well trained in new, specialized skills. At the same time, the persistence of poverty and joblessness among women, minorities, school dropouts, and dislocated workers highlighted the need to help those most at risk gain the skills they needed to become independent, productive members of society.

If we could devise an education and training system to serve these twin objectives—meeting the needs of industry for specific skills right now, and helping those not part of the economic mainstream to find work—then we would be well on our way to meeting our goals of economic innovation and opportunity for all.

That was the philosophy behind a series of innovative programs, starting with Employment and Training Choices, or ET —a new collaboration between state agencies concerned with welfare and those helping industry with their manpower needs.

From Welfare to Work: Employment and Training Choices

The Employment and Training Choices program is a cornerstone of our success in helping Massachusetts citizens become economically self-sufficient. Since the program began in October 1983, more than 43,000 welfare recipients have found full- or part-time employment through ET. Average full-time wages have provided families with incomes that doubled the average welfare grant; and of those who left welfare through the program, 86 percent were still off welfare one year later. In four years, ET has already made a real dent in long-term welfare dependency. And behind the statistics are some incredible human tales.

GETTING RUBY SAMPSON TO THE OPERATING ROOM STAFF

Ruby Sampson, mother of three, had left school in the seventh grade to pick cotton and help raise her twelve younger brothers and sisters. For fourteen years, from 1971 to 1985, she was on welfare. As she says, "I was a wreck. I had all this energy boxed into four walls and no way to let it out." At an ET Choices orientation, Ruby was given a choice of training programs, one of which would qualify her as an operating room technician. Her childhood dream of becoming a doctor resurfaced.

For forty-four weeks, Ruby studied anatomy, physiology, and surgical procedures at the Dimock Community Health Center. This program, cosponsored by five Boston-area hospitals, trains central supply technicians and operating room technicians. ET trainees can enroll in this program; its most famous graduate is Ruby Sampson. The Bay State Skills Corporation runs the program. The private sector puts in two dollars for every one provided by BSSC. Hospitals donate supplies, doctors and nurses donate their time by regularly coming to class and lecturing, and the nurse supervisors who work with the participants for twenty-one weeks of supervision are dedicated and very supportive.

While Sampson studied at Dimock and interned at the Massachusetts General Hospital, ET Choices provided day care for her children and covered her transportation expenses to the hospital. Since October 1986, Ruby Sampson has been an operating room technician at Brigham and Women's, one of the finest teaching hospitals in Boston. She is making more than three times what she did on welfare. Ruby caught the nation's attention when she told a news conference in Washington, D.C.: "The old Ruby is dead, a new Ruby exists."

GETTING DAWN LAWSON TO THE NORTON COMPANY

Dawn Lawson never wanted to turn to welfare but she had no choice; she needed to support herself and her young son. But Dawn was embarrassed to be on welfare because people in the grocery store knew when she was paying with food stamps, and people in the doctor's office could see that she had a Medicaid card. Dawn admits now that she started to think less of herself, feeling that she wasn't smart enough to get a job and be on her own.

After attending a twenty-week ET Choices' clerical and office machine program, she felt confident enough at word processing to apply for a job at Norton Company. Soon Dawn was making three times what she had received on welfare—and she now runs her own business. She is saving money and is hoping to buy a house. "Since I got my job, my life has changed a lot," she says. "I have moved out of public housing, bought a car, and have taken my son on two vacations to Cape Cod." Norton's Thomas Hourihan, vice president of human resources, calls ET Choices, "the best program I have ever been associated with."

These stories could be matched by thousands more. By any count, the numbers are impressive:

- More than eight thousand Massachusetts businesses have hired ET graduates; AT&T Technologies in North Andover has itself hired sixty-one people through ET.
- A significant and growing proportion of ET participants are women with children under the age of six: in the first year of the program, 18 percent of ET participants fell into this category. This figure had more than doubled by the end of the 1986 fiscal year, to 41 percent. The availability of affordable child care has been a crucial factor in enabling these families to become independent of public assistance.
- Minorities now account for 35 percent of all ET placements, compared to 26 percent in each of the first two years of the program; more significantly, minority wage rates have increased dramatically, from 82 percent of the wage rate for white workers in the 1984 fiscal years, to over 96 percent in the most recent fiscal year.
- The average length of stay on the welfare rolls has fallen by 29 percent since December 1982—from an average of forty

months to an average of twenty-eight months. The number of clients who remain on the caseload continuously for five years or more fell by more than 25 percent in three years.

The ET program grew out of an awareness that welfare, while necessary and important in providing temporary help for families in need, can become a spiraling trap which decreases its victims' self-respect and sense of responsibility and increases their dependence. It is not enough simply to give people a monthly stipend. Nor has the workfare trend which requires welfare recipients to work off their welfare check been successful; these programs fail because they do not provide recipients with the skills and confidence for long-run self-sufficiency.

The word "Choices" in the ET program title is significant. ET stresses self-motivated client participation. ET is tailored to the needs of each person. It provides welfare recipients with a route out of poverty by helping them overcome whatever their own barriers to self-sufficiency might be. Barriers include illiteracy, an inability to speak English, insufficient education, a lack of marketable skills or work experience, the high cost and inadequate supply of child care, or the prospect of losing Medicaid.

Assessment and career-planning services are available to clients at all of the local welfare offices. After counseling, an ET participant may choose from a menu of employment programs to meet his or her unique needs:

- Job development and placement activities for individuals who are ready to look for work.
- Career planning for individuals who need guidance in deciding upon a specific employment goal.
- Basic literacy, adult education, general equivalency degree preparation, and English as a second language programs for individuals lacking the basic skills and background necessary to compete in the labor market.
- Skills training for individuals who lack marketable skills and who want to be trained for jobs in a specific field.

- Supported work for individuals who lack work experience and marketable skills and who require a gradual transition to unsubsidized employment. (Supported-work participants often wind up being hired by the firms they train in.)
- Child-care vouchers and transportation reimbursement to remove two major financial disincentives to participating in ET.
- Day-care and Medicaid benefits for up to a year after leaving welfare.

Michael Barone of the *Washington Post* summarized the payback from such investments: "These expensive but temporary services help mothers get hooked on work and help them to do well enough to afford health insurance and child care." [*Washington Post*, 2/10/86]

While all applicants for Aid to Families with Dependent Children (AFDC) are required to register with ET if their children are six years of age or older, we also reach out through the casework system and through an aggressive marketing program to make sure that AFDC clients have every encouragement to use the program. We have made a special effort to reach out to particular recipient groups, including principal earners in two-parent families; women with children between the ages of fourteen and eighteen; teenage dependents; pregnant teenagers and teenage mothers; public housing residents; recipients who have been on the caseload two or more years; and, of course, mothers with children under the age of six who voluntarily choose to enter the program.

For those ET participants seeking skills training, an excellent network of programs is available throughout the state. Many of these are offered by public-private partnerships under the guidance of the Bay State Skills Corporation. One such program is sponsored by the Greater Boston YMCA, through its subsidiary, Training, Inc., and cosponsored by a host of companies including John Hancock Insurance, Bank of Boston, and Brigham and Women's Hospital.

CLIMBING THE SUCCESS PYRAMID AT TRAINING, INC.

Training, Inc., is located in Boston's downtown business district, immediately conveying a sense that it means business. With an 88 percent placement rate after five cycles and an 87 percent retention rate after one year, Training, Inc., fulfills its mission of training the unemployed or underemployed.

The most recent class of men and women ranged in age from seventeen to sixty-two and entered directly from the welfare rolls, the unemployment ranks, or plant closings. Referring agencies paid $3,000 per student (not the full tuition cost)—but they will pay less if the graduate does not get a job.

Training, Inc., provides Boston businesses with well-trained employee candidates who have developed the skills, appearance, and manner appropriate for an office environment, at no cost to the potential employer. They can work well with customers, co-workers, and supervisors; they can manage their time and solve problems. They are enthusiastic, confident, and eager to learn new skills and office procedures.

TI concentrates on preparing people for careers, not just for entry-level positions. Of those who find employment, 93 percent advance through raises, promotions, or new positions. The TI curriculum provides hands-on experience for its thirty or so participants in each cycle. Each classroom is set up so that students learn by doing. The accounting room consists of a large table with thirteen adding machines/calculators spaced around it; the typing room has thirteen typewriters, each set on its own desk; the computer room has thirteen terminals and end tables.

Students are given the message that they are independent learners, working apart from the class but at the same time a part of the larger group. The self-paced work routine varies from an accounting Professional Packet of typical accounting chores at a doctor's, dentist's, and lawyer's office to a simulation exercise called Lester Hill. Here the trainees each apply and are hired for a position in one of six departments in a hotel/motel supply company, and for two weeks perform the duties required of their position. These simulated exercises are augmented by business excursions to local companies, where trainees see people performing business tasks and observe office procedures without fear of making a mistake, asking a dumb question, or being thought of as unproductive.

Everything at TI reinforces the message that success stems more from personal *strengths* than from practical *skills*. A Success Pyramid illustrates the skills TI considers essential for career success, starting at the base with "dependability" and rising to "ability to suggest improvements." A Cycle Chart, for example, lists each trainee by first name and leaves room for the name of his or her first employer to be posted beside it. A variety of industry types offer positions to trainees; many of them are well-known national and local companies. Across from this information about current TI participants is a wall displaying eight-by-ten-inch glossy black-and-white photos of TI graduates in their new jobs. Everyone looks very professional, poised, happy, and productive—an incentive for newcomers to the program or for graduates just entering their new jobs.

The best part of the Training, Inc., story is the people themselves, people who have gained hope along with their skills, self-confidence along with their jobs and earnings.

- Although Susan had been a bank teller before coming to TI, she was very nervous in the program. She had been on welfare for the past ten years and was afraid of stepping out on her own. Her ex-husband resented and discouraged her ambition. Following TI graduation, Susan stepped into a receptionist position at Brigham and Women's in the purchasing department. When TI needed a receptionist for their office, they called in five graduates, one of whom was Susan. She took the job, is now the TI office manager, and actually does some typing instruction. In March 1987, she married Bob, a man she met in her Training, Inc., course.

- Ed has muscular dystrophy and came to TI to develop skills that would enable him to work despite his loss of muscle coordination. A "people person all the way around," he found his first job as a customer service representative at Sperry TopSider, part of the Stride Rite Corporation. He is earning $100 more a week than when he started two years ago and looks forward to a supervisory position in the near future. Ed has contributed artwork and articles for internal corporate newsletters and was recently instrumental in hiring another TI graduate from the last cycle.

- Kathy's son is a hemophiliac, and she had missed a lot of working time caring for him. At TI she was a loner, "a hard worker and quick, but not bright and cheerful." To help Kathy make the transition into the working world, TI hired her as a receptionist. Kathy gained confidence and eventually went to work for the Dana Farber Cancer Institute. She has had two quick raises amounting to more than a 16 percent pay increase. "Now she calls in regularly to see how we're doing, and I can hear the smile in her voice," said Sandy Moore, TI's chief job developer. "Her husband had just been put on unemployment and was thinking about entering one of our cycles."

- Julie made it through TI "by the skin of her teeth. She came in and tried hard but reached a point where her learning capacity froze; she just couldn't remember things or perform machine skills well." TI staff helped her and tried to make the painful learning process easier. Julie refused to give up, entered another training program after graduating from TI, and after a one-and-a-half-year job search, found a job at an investment firm and loves it. Moore says that "Julie's newfound pride in a good day's work made the time and effort building up the skills necessary to procure a job worth it to Julie."

In 1987 a grateful graduate visited TI the day she got her first paycheck and donated half of it on the spot to the program—TI's largest alumni donation yet.

"RISING TIDE" OR "LEAKY BOAT?": CONFIRMING THE VALUE OF ET CHOICES

For every person who leaves welfare permanently through the ET program, the state of Massachusetts saves tens of thousands of dollars. And this does not count the income taxes which will be paid by the workers. Thus, ET saves tax dollars, while providing businesses with badly needed and well-trained employees.

The success of ET Choices has been acclaimed nationwide. But it has also led observers to wonder whether the booming Massachusetts economy would have led to reductions in the welfare rolls anyway, even without the ET program. Was it a matter simply of a "rising tide lifting all boats"? Or were there some "leaky boats" that would have sunk without the state's repair service?

The analytical evidence is clear: ET works. For one thing, we began the program when the unemployment in Massachusetts was over 7 percent. Its success was unquestionably helped by high labor demand in a growth economy, but without ET, many people on welfare would have remained unemployed. In August 1987, the Massachusetts Taxpayers Foundation, a business-supported research group that is often critical of state programs, released an elaborate and rigorous study of ET, concluding:

> So far, the investment in ET has paid off in Massachusetts. The savings to the state far outrun the cost of the program. Financial benefits to recipients are likely to improve, and there are other benefits we can't quantify.
>
> Will ET continue to save money? That's unclear. Those entering the program now need more services than their predecessors,

so the cost will continue to rise. On the other hand, these participants would use more of the state's welfare services, for a longer
period, if they remained on AFDC—so the investment could
continue to pay off.

It is unclear what would happen if unemployment in the
state were to rise significantly . . . But, for now at least, ET
has proven itself an effective money-saver, by cutting a portion
of the state's largest single budget item, human services.
[Massachusetts Taxpayers Foundation report, *Training People to Live
Without Welfare*, August 87]

ET worked because of remarkable collaboration across state
agencies. The Department of Public Welfare depended on other
agencies and programs to develop and offer the training and job
placement for ET participants. Behind the success of ET were
the two major arms of the state's employment and training system—the Bay State Skills Corporation and the local Job Training Partnership Act network. Let's look at how these programs
work for the people and businesses of Massachusetts.

The Bay State Skills Corporation: Advanced Skills for a Changing Economy

In 1978, Massachusetts released a study that projected an increased demand for people in high-technology industries and
the inability of the educational community to meet that demand. In 1981, the Legislature created the Bay State Skills Corporation to build partnerships through which the state and
private industry could jointly fund programs of skills training
consistent with real employment needs. BSSC links providers of
training with providers of jobs. As Caroline Stouffer, head of
ET/Welfare programs for BSSC, said, "We do not train for jobs
which do not exist." Over 90 percent of the graduates of BSSC
get full-time employment in the private sector.

BSSC training covers a wide spectrum of Massachusetts' changing, knowledge-intensive economy. For example, Massasoit Community College in Brockton, with the collaboration of Continental Cablevision, Milton Cablesystems Corporation, and Campbell Communications, trained twenty-five cable television line service technicians. Digital Equipment Corporation and Analogics, two of our computer giants, joined BSSC to fund the start-up of an industrial robotics center at the University of Lowell. Quincy Junior College joined with six local eye care clinics to train twenty-five optometric technicians. In Western Massachusetts, Berkshire Community College teamed with Berkshire Medical Center, Hillcrest Hospital, North Adams Regional Hospital, and Fairview Hospital to train sixteen respiratory therapy technicians. In each case, the state's dollars were more than matched by the sponsoring companies.

BSSC is known worldwide and it has briefed visitors from China, France, Great Britain, Australia, and even Japan on its highly successful approach to training. The states of Washington, Kentucky, Minnesota, and Florida have created similar programs, and Senators Paul Tsongas and Edward Kennedy introduced a U.S. Skills Act in the U.S. Senate, for a national network of state skills corporations. In 1987 BSSC was one of three Massachusetts programs to reach the final round in the Innovations in State and Local Government Awards Program, sponsored by The Ford Foundation and the John F. Kennedy School of Government at Harvard University.

Over its first six years of operation, BSSC has built public-private partnerships in an ever-broader range of advanced technologies. General Electric's much-heralded "Factory of the Future" in Lynn was among many major employers joining with the BSSC to train their workers in new technologies. The list of BSSC partnerships reads like a Who's Who of the *Fortune* 500. The $73,000 contract BSSC gave the Growth Opportunity Alliance of Greater Lawrence to train quality expediters was matched by over $200,000 from Digital Equipment, Compugraphic, Gillette, McCord Winn, Honeywell, Gould, Shawsheen Printing, and Alco Electronic Products. Overall, BSSC has helped to bring together over six hundred companies and two hundred educational institutions. Executive Director Susan Moulton summarized BSSC's philosophy in her letter to Massachusetts business people: "If you are a company that cannot find skilled workers, call me."

The Bay State Skills Corporation has been a happy marriage of customized training for business and help for people facing special barriers to finding work. It has made sure that people are trained for jobs that employers really need to fill.

Local Training for Local Needs: From JTPA to New Jobs

The other major arm of our employment-and-training system is a network of services established under the federal Job Training Partnership Act, or JTPA. Established by the Congress in 1982 as a successor to the old CETA program, JTPA shifted much of the responsibility for employment and training policy from the federal level to the nation's governors and legislatures.

While state governments were given the role of setting basic policies and performance standards, the design and implementation of employment-and-training programs was placed closer to the grass roots. By the spring of 1983, the Commonwealth's employment and training system had been reorganized into fifteen Service Delivery Areas based on metropolitan and regional economies. In each of these areas, a team of business, labor, education, and social service leaders was recruited to the policy-making board, the so-called Private Industry Council.

The Job Training Partnership Act is a great improvement over its federal predecessors, but it still does not guarantee that our array of employment-and-training resources will be as well co-ordinated, or as accessible to businesses and potential trainees, as we need. We are now working to change the face of our JTPA system—bringing more of the employment-and-training network under its umbrella, and marketing it aggressively to small businesses and the public at large. A first step was to give the system a new, less bureaucratic name—MassJobs.

The value of a more inclusive, coordinated, and accessible employment-and-training system has already been demonstrated all across Massachusetts. JTPA funds, when combined with other public and private resources, can be flexible enough to serve single companies, such as Richdale Stores; groups of companies, such as the fiber optics firms in southern Worcester County; or whole industries, such as machining and metal-working.

CONVENIENT TRAINING IN A CONVENIENCE STORE

Richdale Stores is the retail arm of West Lynn Creamery, a dairy products firm with one thousand Massachusetts employees. West Lynn enjoys a reputation for being a forward-thinking company; it was one of the first companies in New England to take advantage of International Paper's offer to put pictures of missing children on milk cartons.

Like other retail and fast-food businesses in Massachusetts in the mid-1980s, Richdale Stores has had a difficult time recruiting and keeping qualified personnel to manage their stores. It was this situation that led a much larger Massachusetts company, Dunkin' Donuts, to establish its own innovative school, Dunkin' Donuts University, to service the training needs of its nearly fifteen hundred stores. But as a smaller company, Richdale could not afford to build and staff its own training facility.

A few years ago, Arthur Papathanasi, the company's vice president of finance, was discussing this situation with his friend, Harry McCabe. McCabe was the director of the North Shore Employment and Training Program, the regional JTPA operation in the area. McCabe suggested that Richdale let him use an operating store to provide a classroom and on-the-job training for unemployed people. Papathanasi immediately saw the advantages for Richdale Stores.

At the same time, a nonprofit development organization, Step-Up-With-Lynn, approached Richdale about locating a store in a section of Lynn that they were hoping to revitalize. Richdale took a lease in a Step-Up-With-Lynn building which helped to improve the neighborhood and encouraged other stores to move in. It did not take long for the Richdale store to show a profit. This is the store where Richdale let McCabe set up his classroom. Richdale's motives were twofold: providing a community service by helping to revitalize a downtown area and developing an effective way to find and train good people for their stores. A portion of the revenues from this unusual working classroom goes back to Richdale for inventory, a portion is invested in the store, and the final piece goes to match the federal JTPA funds.

Richdale provided training materials and supervision, and McCabe developed a sixteen-week training program for older workers and displaced homemakers. Three levels of training prepare people for jobs as an inventory control clerk, assistant manager, or manager. Two spin-off programs train for bookkeeping and maintenance.

Since this training program was the first of its kind, it attracted attention from other convenience store owners throughout the country. In the program's first two years, graduates were successfully placed as managers of Richdale Stores, as well as cashiers and clerks in other retail stores. One person even started his own business.

COOPERATION AMONG COMPETITORS: THE FIBER OPTICS PROGRAM

In late 1984, Governor Dukakis called together the leaders of the most successful fiber-optics firms in Central Massachusetts. Because the industry is so competitive, owners of these firms tend to shy away from contact with one another. But Dukakis got the leaders of these companies talking. With the aid of the South-bridge Chamber of Commerce, the MacKinnon Training Center, and the local Private Industry Council, the governor and the industry leaders soon recognized that the common thread that united these diverse firms was the need for skilled workers. Within months after their discussions began, four companies had pledged equipment, materials, and personnel to teach a ten-week fiber-optics program at the MacKinnon Training Center, using the group's resources in combination with JTPA funds.

The MacKinnon Training Center is housed in an old redbrick neighborhood school building in Southbridge. When the building became available in 1979, Executive Director John Dvareckas at last had a home for a training center that could work with local businesses to assess and meet their needs for qualified people.

Using JTPA funds to administer the fiber-optics program, the center staff began the difficult task of screening some seventy applicants. After personal interviews and standardized tests, twenty applicants were chosen for the program. Seven of these were AFDC mothers. All were JTPA-eligible people, ranging in ages from eighteen to forty-four. Half of the class was female, and there was one minority student. Some students in the course continued to collect unemployment insurance and AFDC mothers collected their welfare checks.

In the fall of 1985, the fiber-optics program began. One counselor at the training center remembered that the students were quite anxious during the first class—after all, many had dropped out of school and others had not been in school for years. But quickly the tone of voices and the expressions on the faces of the students changed; they were excited about learning. And it was no wonder, for these students were receiving instruction from dedicated, knowledgeable people from the fiber-optics industry. Students found Dr. Walter Siegmund of Reichert Scientific Instruments and Fiber Optics particularly inspirational. Siegmund treated the students as if they were in college, pushing them to do more and more difficult math problems. The students responded. In ten weeks they received the equivalent of six months of on-the-job training, but more important, they gained confidence in themselves.

The companies involved in the program got first choice at hiring the students. Starting salaries for the graduates ranged from $5.50 to $7.00 per hour. But these statistics tell only part of the story. Takeshi Okamura, a resident of Sturbridge, moved to this country from Japan six months before the training began. Okamura had had a hard time finding a job. "The fiber-optics course gave me a really good opportunity to get into American industry," explains Okamura. After graduation, Okamura accepted a job with Galileo, one of the four company sponsors of the training program.

Producing a work force able to take today's jobs is one important use of the JTPA programs. But, in Massachusetts, we wanted to go one step further—to anticipate the retraining needs of changing industries in order to be ready for *tomorrow's* jobs.

ANTICIPATING RETRAINING NEEDS: HELP FOR MATURE INDUSTRIES

The Machine Action Project (MAP) in Western Massachusetts is one of three demonstrations in the state's Cooperative Regional Industrial Laboratory program, or CRIL. CRIL is an experimental economic development program that focuses on job retention and creation in mature industries threatened by foreign competition. Emphasizing regional concentrations of companies and workers, CRIL projects try to blend the expertise of the work force with professional skills in management, engineering, and marketing.

CRIL is sponsored by the Massachusetts Industrial Services Program, the state's lead agency for helping mature industries. It is funded through a combination of state and JTPA resources. CRIL projects are carried out through contracts with local economic development or job-training agencies, and each of the CRILs is guided by a board that includes labor, business, educational, and community leadership.

The Machine Action Project was initiated by the Hampden County Employment and Training Consortium to address a clear and pressing issue. Since 1980, six thousand jobs had been lost in the machining and metalworking industries of the Greater Springfield area. When the project staff undertook an industry survey and needs analysis, they found an industry more diverse and extensive than they had expected—but one with real problems.

In 1986, there were 338 firms in the county, ranging in size from 1 employee to over 500. The industry employed approximately 15,000 people in the Springfield area, two-thirds of whom worked in firms with fewer than 25 employees. Most of these companies produced no proprietary products, leaving them at the mercy of major corporations who contract with them for specific machining work or for defense contracts. A number of companies were up for sale, raising the specter of plant closures under new management. Furthermore, the weakest segment of the industry was the foundries. In three years, close to 500 foundry jobs were lost, nearly half the total. These workers were doubly at risk—the industry was declining and they had few transferable skills.

Despite these difficulties, the potential for growth did exist. Several shops had the latest machine-tool technology available in their plant. Many were qualified to meet all of the inspection demands that industry is now placing on contracted machining work. Several firms had diversified, reducing their dependency on defense-related work and broadening their base beyond a few major customers. But the major impediment to growth was the lack of a trained, multiskilled work force. Workers who had lost their jobs in recent plant closings did not have the skills necessary to fill available openings in the precision machining industry. Smaller shops needed more flexible workers, people who are trained to operate a half-dozen machines, rather than just a single machine which was sufficient in order to work in larger companies in the past. At the same time, a perception in the community that the industry was dying led to declining enrollments in machining programs offered in the region's vocational schools. New skills and an industry boost were needed.

By 1987, the Machine Action Project was ready to begin retraining dislocated workers in the skills that would contribute to the industry's revitalization. In addition to training, the MAP staff was prepared to serve as a marketing resource for the industry in Hampden County, helping local machine shops find new business in other areas of the country that use contract machining services.

Building Toward Tomorrow:
Public Higher Education

In Massachusetts we believe that higher education is a key to economic innovation and growth. In the past, private universities had been preeminent in Massachusetts. As one observer put it: "Without MIT, Route 128 would be simply two lanes running in each direction." But over the last decade, the *public* higher education system began to play an ever-greater role. We have already seen in the case of the University of Lowell how vital a linkage can arise between excellence at one of our public institutions and the growth of the area economy. A different kind of example that makes the same point is the connection between the Millitech Corporation and our flagship campus, the University of Massachusetts at Amherst.

PUBLIC UNIVERSITIES AND THE ENTREPRENEURIAL SPIRIT: MILLITECH AND UMASS—AMHERST

The Pioneer Valley, eighty-five miles west of Boston, is an attractive place for engineers and scientists. Standing on the southern outskirts of Amherst, you can look in one direction and see a thick forest; in the other direction lies a pasture which fades back into the Holyoke range of hills. Look north and there's a hillside orchard. A glance east carries you through a broad valley to the Putnam Hills. The campus of the University of Massachusetts—Amherst operates one of the largest educational programs for microwave engineering in the country.

Millitech is a rapidly growing company that thrives on this uncommon combination of environmental and educational resources. It is located in South Deerfield, ten miles north of Amherst on the Connecticut River. Millitech makes and sells components, assemblies, and subsystems operating in the millimeter and submillimeter regions of the electromagnetic spectrum.

The company was launched in the late 1960s by Dr. Richard Huguenin. Huguenin, who was educated at MIT and Harvard, accepted a position at UMass—Amherst in the early 1970s to found and run the Radio-Astronomy Observatory. When Huguenin and four of his colleagues discovered that the equipment necessary to pursue their research at the observatory was not commercially available, they decided to start Millitech. Forced to develop the needed equipment themselves, they were initially sponsored by the state and by the National Science Foundation. As they began to receive requests from other companies to develop equipment, they began to discuss the prospects of starting their own company. Six years after it was launched, the company employed seventy people, of whom thirty are engineers and scientists. Six of them are Ph.D.'s, and fifteen hold master's degrees.

According to Huguenin, Millitech is essentially "a single product company" which addresses a number of different markets.

By identifying niches within the defense electronics market, the company offers unique solutions to defense problems. Because millimeter waves are ten times smaller than microwaves, millimeter components are smaller as well—millimeter radars can fit in the bottom of a coffee cup. At the same time, the company also finds innovative niches in the consumer market, like the application of wave technology to the problem of guiding airplanes through fog. Frederick Smith, CEO of Federal Express, for example, is particularly interested in Millitech's work becaues of his need to deliver packages in all weather conditions.

Huguenin describes the culture of the company as "very much like it was in the university. No one pays attention to dress and other outward manifestations of appearance." Employees, he said, were "enthusiastic about their work. At six P.M., the parking lot is still at least one-third full. People enjoy what they are doing."

It is important to him that employees have a great deal of freedom to be creative at all levels, including the engineers, scientists, and manufacturing people. If people have ideas, they come to him or the other managers. Or an idea comes up and "we stand around a machine and talk." Millitech people pay attention to high-quality performance and reliability of their products. "People take pride in the engineering and technical aspects of their work, but there is the added need to meet customer specifications." Millitech gives small awards ($100) for the publication of articles, a recognition that "publishing is important to Millitech," just as it is at the university.

As a way of tapping new knowledge from outside the company, employees are encouraged to attend scientific and professional meetings. The development of joint projects with organizations like NASA is also a way for Millitech's scientists and engineers to solve problems and gain new knowledge in the process.

Huguenin is very clear about the reasons for Millitech's success. The single most important reason is the state's educational facilities, both universities and high schools. "In the long term," he maintains, "the educational climate set by the state is a critical issue." It made sense for Millitech to stay in the area since some of the company's associates are still connected to UMass through research and teaching.

Millitech recruits from all over the country, and it helps that UMass operates one of the largest training programs for microwave engineering in the country. It was more difficult, at first, to recruit skilled machinists. So Millitech turned to the Bay State Skills Corporation, and BSSC helped train its machinists.

The twenty-seven public institutions of higher learning Massachusetts supports range from the state university campuses at Amherst, Boston, and Worcester, to the regional universities in Lowell and Southeastern Massachusetts, to a half-dozen four-year state colleges, to specialized maritime and arts schools, to fifteen two-year community colleges serving every region of the state. Enrollments in the state system have quintupled in the last twenty-five years. More than 60 percent of our state's residents who attend college are enrolled in a Massachusetts public college or university.

From 1983 to 1986, Massachusetts increased its financial support for public higher education by a greater proportion than any other state in the nation. We have increased faculty salaries by an average of 33 percent; today, salaries at the University of Massachusetts are in the top 10 percent of faculty salaries nationwide. We quadrupled state scholarship assistance from $19 million in 1982 to $75 million in 1986—to ensure that the door of opportunity would be open to all our students. Then, in February 1987, I announced a seven-year, $954 million capital plan to modernize, expand, and upgrade the public colleges and universities of Massachusetts. New campuses in Lowell and Lawrence will join the ones we have already built in Lynn and Roxbury as centers of regional and community growth. New laboratories and computer systems will reinvigorate the entire system.

The Next Generation: Educating and Caring for Our Children

Our children are our future. Tomorrow's work force is already visible today, in the toddlers and sixth graders and high-school students of America. How they are treated and what they learn today will determine whether industry can find its talent and its brainpower tomorrow.

Attention to the education and care of children not only builds a foundation for the future, it also meets the needs of the parents who are today's work force. Parents care about their children's education, and for the highly skilled professionals responsible for business innovation, this is often the major factor behind their choice to settle in an area.

Dick Johnson, the mayor of Taunton (himself a former teacher), understands the importance of good schools in attracting businesses to his community. Companies considering Taunton set tough standards for the city's schools. MetroByte asked about Taunton's curriculum in science, math, and computers. GTE specifically asked, "How many computers do you have in your schools?" Johnson recalls that he personally went into every school and counted every computer. But the schools have changed dramatically in the years from 1982 to 1987. Johnson explained: "Five years ago, we had one library for the school system; now we have a library in every school. Five years ago we had a few computers in the high school; now we have computers in all the schools. We now have a schedule to update the curriculum: once every five years we completely redo a subject area. This is the fifth year, so we are now back in the beginning of the cycle." Johnson knows that businesses do not move into a new area that lacks excellent schools.

Public elementary and secondary schools are the foundation upon which our hopes for a skilled and knowledgeable work force rest. In 1985, the Massachusetts Legislature enacted, and I signed into law, the Commonwealth's sweeping Education

Improvement Act. The bill starts with two basic educational building blocks: our school districts and our teachers. Equal Education Opportunity Grants address a long-standing problem—the inability of poorer communities to provide the necessary resources for a first-rate educational system. Now, districts spending less than 85 percent of the state average receive special state aid to close the gap. A series of new programs is making teaching an honored and valued profession once again, one our young people can look forward to entering. For example:

- *Horace Mann Teacher Program.* Each year individual teachers can apply to their local school committee for a Horace Mann grant. The grants, which can pay up to $2,500 per year, reward teachers for assuming expanding responsibilities in areas from teacher training to school-home-community liaison projects.
- *Lucretia Crocker Fellowship Program.* In 1986–87, we awarded Lucretia Crocker Fellowships to sixteen outstanding teachers. Under the leadership of Commissioner of Education Harold Raynolds, we established the program to support teacher-initiated educational reform and to improve the conditions of teaching. The sixteen fellows spent the year holding workshops in schools throughout the state with fellow teachers about the innovative and successful curriculum which the fellows had developed. One fellow called the year, "the most personally and professionally rewarding experience" of his life.

The bill encourages our schools to embrace a more rigorous, innovative, and demanding curriculum. Four different assessment and testing programs monitor how our pupils, teachers, administrators, and entire districts are performing on a regular basis. Educational technology grants support a strong effort in computer and technological literacy—an obvious need if our state is to maintain its edge in the world's knowledge-based economy. Hundreds of grass-roots School Improvement Councils are encouraging creativity and innovation in every school in Massachusetts. Each council receives $10 per pupil per year. With the school students, principal, teachers, parents, and a community representative as members, each council has the breadth of support and the creativity to do something special.

Partnerships for Day Care: Model Programs in Action

Massachusetts' employers have come to recognize what thousands of working families have already discovered—that quality, affordable day care is an economic necessity. Almost 20 percent of the mothers in the state provide the sole support for their families, and over half of Massachusetts mothers with children under six work full-time.

One of the economic realities in a state with an unemployment rate of 3 percent is that two questions—how do we extend opportunity to all families, and how do we help expanding businesses find the workers they need—have the same answer: day care.

One thing is also crystal clear—the public treasury cannot pay for all the day care we need. The Commonwealth already subsidizes day care for the children of low- and moderate-income working families. But employers must be deeply involved as well. In January 1985, I established the Governor's Day Care Partnership to increase the supply and improve the quality of affordable day care for the families of the Commonwealth. I pledged that over the next two years we would take a leadership role on the child-care issue by encouraging business, labor, local government, schools, higher education, day-care providers, and advocates to work together as partners in each community.

With the help of the State Legislature, we have established a network of regional child-care resources and referral agencies to provide technical assistance to employers and families and encourage more privately financed day care. There are now twelve regional centers serving every city and town in Massachusetts. These centers help link parents, employers, and providers in ways that meet specific local needs. In Lawrence, for example, the resource agency worked with a local manufacturer to open a work-site day-care center, while in Holyoke the agency led a family-day-care recruitment drive.

We are encouraging businesses to provide as much employer-sponsored day care as possible, including on-site facilities whenever practicable. At present, ninety-nine Massachusetts companies are supporting day-care centers, including sixty who do so on-site. In Worcester, a local insurance company started a day-care referral service for employees that included funding for seven local day-care providers willing to give the children of company employees enrollment preference.

In 1986, the state and one of its largest private sector employers joined hands to create an unprecedented $1.5 million pool to help finance new day-care initiatives. The Massachusetts Industrial Finance Agency announced a $750,000 loan fund for work-site day-care centers, while the New England Telephone Company announced a $750,000 grant for nonprofit day-care centers. These accomplishments could not have been achieved by government alone. Involving employers has been the key to our Day Care Partnership.

At the same time, Massachusetts has committed new public resources to quality day care. Salaries of child-care workers in centers with state contracts and rates for family day care providers have been raised substantially in two years—an investment we simply must make if decent child care is to be available to thousands of working families. We have also increased by 35 percent the number of state-assisted day-care places available to the children of ET participants—one of the principal reasons for that program's success.

As the largest employer in the state, Massachusetts is also working hard to be a model employer itself. In almost forty state office buildings and facilities and public college campuses, we have created day-care centers to meet the needs of our employees. We have at the State House, for example, the Commonwealth's Children's Center, a parent-controlled, independent, nonprofit organization that offers care for up to forty-six children from infants to five-year-olds.

We have also brought our public employee unions into the partnership. During the most recent round of collective bargaining, we created joint labor-management committees to assist in establishing and promoting the use of child-care facilities in state-owned buildings. More significantly, for the first time in the state's collective bargaining history, we set aside $225,000 to implement the initiatives recommended by the committees.

CHAPTER FIVE

Targets for Opportunity: Building Strong Regional Economies

The national media may see the entire Massachusetts economy through the prism of booming growth in downtown Boston and on Route 128. But even in a small state like ours there are regional economies rooted in an earlier time that look and feel very different.

During all of my years as governor, and especially during these past five years, a primary concern for me has been that economic growth be encouraged throughout the commonwealth, not just in metropolitan Boston. Business leaders recognize this challenge too; as a vice president of Teradyne, a Boston-based high-tech firm, commented, "It makes no sense for high-tech companies to pile plants on top of one another in ten percent of the state's area."

I have always thought that building strong local and regional economies was an important job for my state's public and private leaders. But when I was running for governor in 1982, we were in the midst of a national recession and the impact of those hard times on the less favored regions of Massachusetts was especially moving. I'll never forget marching in the annual North Adams Fall Foliage Parade that year, when unemployment in the northern Berkshires was 20 percent and laid-off workers—proud men and women with children to feed—called out to me that they needed jobs and hope. It was a scene from the Great Depression.

In that same campaign, I took the State House press corps on a tour of New Bedford to show them that Southeastern Massachusetts was working hard to forge a comeback. But times were very tough. It was clear that if Southeastern Massachusetts was to make it into the state's economic mainstream, it would take every ounce of public and private effort we could muster.

Two years later, when the state's overall economic performance had begun to revive, the underlying contrasts were still acute. During the Christmas holidays of 1984, the shopping malls of Boston's western suburbs—where unemployment was 2 percent and traffic was all but unbearable—had to bus in twelve hundred working people from the Athol-Orange area, a pocket of old mill towns fifty miles to the west. These people, many of them housewives bringing home an extra seasonal paycheck, found work for Christmas, and that was good. But the difference between leaving home to find a job and having a future in a healthy and growing regional economy was plain for all to see.

I gave my Development Cabinet a mission: to reach out to the leadership of every troubled area in Massachusetts—business, labor, education, and government—and help them forge a strategy to create innovation, opportunity, and growth. We pledged our full array of public investment programs to these regional efforts. We were determined to blend and tailor our contributions so that the full impact of our partnership with area leaders would be more than the sum of its parts. And we gave these special regions a name—Targets for Opportunity.

Challenge in the Southeast

We began in Southeastern Massachusetts—an area barely fifty miles from Boston that had suffered from so much neglect that in 1982 the then-secretary of economic affairs had called it "the end of the universe." On January 20, 1983, in just my second week back in office, I brought my Development Cabinet and other key state officials to Southeastern Massachusetts University for an economic summit conference with area leaders. Together, we laid out an agenda for action that was concrete and ambitious. It reflected the priorities of the region's mayors, educators, CEOs, and labor leaders. Five years later, employment in Southeastern Massachusetts has soared. Public and private investment is in full swing; one can feel and sense the pride and confidence and hope of its citizens. The course on which we embarked that day in January 1983 has served the area's people well.

All of the initiatives discussed so far in this book have found their own carefully tailored expression in Southeastern Massachusetts. Our programs for investing in creative entrepreneurship and new technologies have been used again and again—from a regional Marine Sciences Center of Excellence to an industrial park in Taunton that has become a national success story. Creative companies are applying the latest technologies to products as diverse as draperies, cranberries, and photovoltaic cells. At New Bedford's Morse Cutting Tools, a century-old mainstay of manufacturing excellence, we worked for four years to prevent a liquidation and help launch a reorganized, recapitalized enterprise.

Our enthusiasm for rebuilding the fabric of this Commonwealth's older communities has left its mark in Fall River, where the heritage state park I announced ten years ago has become the anchor of a far-reaching revitalization plan for the waterfront and the downtown. The new open-space bill I signed last fall contains the funds for a heritage state park in New Bedford, whose downtown and waterfront combine a historic whaling district of national significance with a rebounding commercial center and the nation's busiest fishing port. The commercial buildings surrounding Taunton's picture-book downtown green are being refurbished and restored through the combined efforts of the city, her business community, and the state. And virtually every major community in Southeastern Massachusetts has joined the Massachusetts Housing Partnership—with results already in hand.

Alongside literally dozens of state infrastructure investments designed to accelerate growth, Massachusetts is investing with equal commitment in the region's quality of life. We are expanding the public's share of beaches, parks, and boating facilities on the region's glistening coastline. We are helping Brockton, New Bedford, and Fall River spruce up their historic Olmsted Parks. We have used our farmland development rights program—not to mention our investments in a resurgent cranberry industry—to keep agriculture alive and well in Southeastern Massachusetts.

Our commitment to invest in people matters a great deal here. When plants have closed in this mature industrial region, we have been there to help the workers get the training and placement assistance they need to land new jobs. The area is almost wholly dependent on public institutions of higher learning, and we have responded with major new investments in the capital plant and program budgets of Southeastern Massachusetts University, Bridgewater State College, and three strong community colleges. We have established a new Science Center at Southeastern Massachusetts University and a new Business Technology Center at Bristol Community College. The Bay State Skills Corporation has scored some of its finest successes with growing Southeastern Massachusetts companies. More recently we have established a model customized training system called MassJobs Southeast.

No part of this undertaking has been done by state government alone. Without the determination, know-how, and optimism of the people of Southeastern Massachusetts—and without a strong Massachusetts economy looking for places to grow —Southeastern Massachusetts would still be reeling. But the Commonwealth has been a key player in the area's renaissance and an ally at every step of the way. No project better embodies the relationship than the development of Myles Standish Industrial Park.

Bringing Business to Southeastern Massachusetts: Myles Standish Industrial Park

Taunton is an industrial town whose old firms made steel, locomotives, gears, and silverware. In the 1960s and 1970s, many struggled, and some closed or moved away. The once-gracious parks and old mansions housing turn-of-the-century industrialists had long been neglected. The city was in a rut.

In 1977, the Commonwealth transferred to the city of Taunton four hundred acres of surplus state land to create the Myles Standish Industrial Park—a badly needed regional magnet for industrial growth. The site had housed a prisoner-of-war camp during World War II and later a mental hospital. In addition to transferring the land, we helped the city get a $380,000 Economic Development Administration grant for new sewer lines and roads.

That same year, construction began on a long-decayed portion of the state's interstate highway system. For we had managed to design, fund, and clear the right-of-way for the so-called missing link of Interstate I-495, to connect Taunton, the rest of Southeastern Massachusetts, and Cape Cod with the interstate network.

Where that highway passes through Taunton, the state designed an interchange that would ensure good access to the planned industrial park. "I remember coming out here one cold day in 1977 with Fred Salvucci, the transportation secretary, and drawing on a piece of paper exactly the way we wanted the Taunton interchange laid out, so it would serve the industrial park," said Alden Raine, my director of economic development.

In 1983, that highway was open, and two hundred acres of Myles Standish were available for industrial use. But there were only two plants—and early that year, one of them closed, when General Mills decided to move an electronic game factory of its Parker Brothers' subsidiary to Mexico. Unemployment in Taunton in the spring of 1983 was nearly 14 percent.

We rolled up our sleeves and went to work with Mayor Dick Johnson and the people of Taunton. When we heard that Surrey Industries, Inc., a newly formed plastic bag manufacturing company, was about to close a deal to start production in Newport News, Virginia, we called the Surrey partners in for a meeting. They were just seventy-two hours from signing the agreement in Virginia when company officials were shown the vacant Parkers Brothers' building and decided it was suitable. I phoned General Mills to urge a compromise on its selling price and, within twenty-four hours, got expedited MIFA approval of a $1.9 million industrial development bond to finance the deal. Surrey brought over two hundred new jobs to Southeastern Massachusetts.

That was just the beginning for Myles Standish. We invested heavily in the park's streets, sidewalks, and sewers. We promoted Myles Standish as a gateway to the abundant land and high-quality work force of Southeastern Massachusetts. When a resurgent Massachusetts economy needed a new direction to grow, Myles Standish Industrial Park was ready.

Today, fifty-four new plants are open or under construction in Myles Standish. They will employ nearly four thousand men and women. They range from Kopin Industries—one of our most promising new photovoltaic producers—to a new GTE plant with eight hundred employees, from dental and medical suppliers to a lumber distributor and a glove manufacturer. I asked John Fan, the young entrepreneur behind Kopin Industries to meet me in my office. His children were going to the same school in Brookline, Massachusetts, that I had attended as a boy. Fan recalls that "the governor had heard about the company and sold me on Taunton, putting together a very nice package for us, including a five-hundred-thousand-dollar subsidized loan."

Land in the park that cost $12,000 an acre in 1982 was going for $39,000 by 1985 and $60,000 by 1987. The original 200-acre Standish Park was filled by 1986, and seventeen more firms were waiting for buildings to be completed in a 125-acre addition. Plants in the original park were assisted by a total of $60 million in industrial revenue land financing backed by MIFA. The best news for the citizens of Taunton: unemployment in Taunton had dropped to 2.8 percent by the fall of 1987.

CURTAINS, CRANBERRIES, AND BATHYTHERMOGRAPHS: REGIONWIDE INNOVATION AND DIVERSITY

The Chace/Roommaker Curtain Company, a division of the Seneca Textile Home Furnishings Group, received $1.8 million in Urban Development Action Grant funds in 1984 for innovations that modernized a declining business and brought it back to profitability. Company officials tell us that a significant part of their recent success grew out of Massachusetts' commitment to renewing the textile industry in Fall River. This has created a kind of vitality and excitement that feeds Chance/Roommaker's vision of its own future, as well as the future of its area and industry.

The vitality shows up the minute a visitor enters a Chace/Roommaker facility. In the middle of an advanced manufacturing facility with the best automated equipment, in an open office on the shop floor, sits Margaret Almeida, the creative heart of the company. Almeida's designs, coupled with new manufacturing technology, have proved to be a winning combination. The Chace/Roommaker story demonstrates how public resources can combine with private initiatives to revitalize a mature industry in a targeted region.

The Seneca Textile Home Furnishings Group is a curtain-producing subsidiary of New York–based United Merchants and Manufacturing. Seneca has a weaving plant in Georgia and three plants in Fall River, including the Chace Mills Curtain Company, the Roommaker Curtain Company, and the Arkwright Finishing Plant. These four plants, and two warehouses in Fall River, form the Chace/Roommaker Curtain Company of the Seneca Group, employing fourteen hundred and generating 1986 revenues in eight figures. The Chace/Roommaker Company represents a 1985 consolidation of two separate companies as a response to changes in the customer market.

For decades, Chace/Roommaker's primary customer was Sears Roebuck. Sears largely controlled its relationship to the Fall River plants, instructing and directing the manufacturer to produce curtains with the styles, colors, and packaging that it specified, based on Sears' marketing studies. At times Chace/Roommaker committed as much as 100 percent of its production to fill Sears orders, while maintaining a relatively small line of its own.

The standard silk screening process used by Chace/Roommaker was efficient for the long runs required by Sears; but it was to prove a liability as the market in general and Sears in particular created a new demand on curtain suppliers to produce a larger number of short runs.

In the Fall River textile community, Chace/Roommaker had noted the technological advances that made many of its competitors showcases for the modern textile plant. However, it had not kept up with the industry for a number of reasons. One was the long-standing, stable, and profitable relationship with Sears. Another was the high levels of commitment between management and labor. The personnel levels of 220 management and 1,200 skilled and unskilled workers had remained essentially unchanged for decades, the plants proudly pointed out the numerous supervisors who have been with the company for over twenty years. The company could also avoid change because unlike the others, which had been adversely affected by imports, the curtain business had not faced a similar threat.

Then, in mid-1984, Sears suddenly abandoned its marketing and design operations and announced its intention to order directly from suppliers' own lines. This meant that in order to compete with bids from other manufacturers for the Sears business, or any business for that matter, Chace/Roommaker had to find a way—quickly—to produce top-quality designs and to market them effectively. The very survival of the company was at stake.

But facing a competitive market with a completely inadequate marketing and design capability was only one issue. Chace/Roommaker had the equally thorny problem of meeting the increasing customer demand for large numbers of relatively short runs. Furthermore, upgrading the Arkwright Finishing Plant's outdated technology would be expensive and a threat to the traditional stability and commitment of company personnel.

Stirred by a threat to its survival, Chace/Roommaker rapidly undertook a wide variety of innovations in structure, process, equipment, and personnel policies that permitted the company to match its competitors and overcome its traditional methods and perspective. The first step was to hire a merchandising manager in the fall of 1984 to promote a shift from dependency upon Sears to independence in the open market. The major targets in the industry were discount and upscale stores, which had become the market's primary volume customers.

At the same time, a number of design people were hired, including Margaret Almeida, whose creative talents were both supported and displayed in the new marketing strategies. To help match Almeida's creative abilities with the production capabilities of the company, Seneca in 1985 merged the formerly separate "cut and sew" Chace Mills Curtain Company with Roommaker Curtain Company. Almeida was given "the highest level of autonomy in the company" to produce her designs. Constructing her office as an open stall on the production floor, she displayed her creations on its walls so that passing personnel could review them informally and give her feedback. She also consulted regularly with engineers to monitor the production implications of her designs.

Chace/Roommaker began to invest in the latest technology at all of its Fall River installations. It wanted to bring curtain production up to industry standards of turnaround responsiveness to reduce limitations on design created by production engineering, as well. It also decided to develop an integrated design/manufacturing process. In collaboration with IRIS and ICONICS, two Massachusetts firms that develop software and equipment for such undertakings, Chace/Roommakers' innovative process put under the control of a single designer many of the steps that were relegated to scattered and labor-intensive consecutive processes under silk screening.

From a large data bank of images based on photographs, outlines, or patterns, the designer can create the basis of a new product print. Then, working from a CRT screen, the designer may choose colors for the print from a palette of sixteen million shades. In the final step, the designer instructs the equipment to print directly onto fabric, offering immediate feedback on the effort with an inexpensive, single-print run. Modifications in shading, tint, or outline may be made quickly and easily, with the same direct-feedback process giving the designer complete knowledge of the effects of modifications. The effect is the equivalent to a computer-based painter's having the ability to produce the exact painting desired, and then running off an unlimited number of copies.

These technological advances came both from trade shows and a clear knowledge of competitors, policies and processes, gained through an open exchange of information and a problem-solving relationship between local competing firms. An operating assumption underlying such a relationship was that there is enough business for everyone, and nothing is to be lost by competitors' collaborating in the areas of technical advances and modernization.

The company's location in Fall River materially contributed to such relationships with local competitors; informal lunch meetings generated significant information about marketing and production policy as well as current innovations. It is a particular characteristic of the Fall River intercorporate community that many relationships cross company boundaries, and talking shop in the city's gathering places provides the benefits of the free exchange of creative thinking, new technological information, and market trends.

Thus, it was relatively easy for Chace/Roommaker people to see what was necessary in the way of technology. What makes their story particularly significant is that this subsidiary with a relatively conservative history decided to take modernization a step further and develop its own innovative process. At this point, state financing tools became critical.

The financial hurdles were managed in part through a contact in Fall River's Economic Development Office. The Chace Mills general manager learned of the industrial revenue bond program, a lead that produced an essential $2.4 million financing package for both the Chace/Roommaker merger and expensive modernization of the Arkwright Finishing Plant. Fall River, which has a 100 percent record of success in obtaining IRBs, provided an independent consultant to guide the company's IRB application. This, in addition to a long-standing relationship with the Bank of New England, made obtaining the IRB a relatively smooth process.

For the Chace/Roommaker management, winning the IRB made the corporate parent in New York take notice. As a result, the modernization effort was financed primarily from within. However, the IRB was a critical step in the larger process of winning financial backing. Looking toward the future, Chace/Roommaker is contemplating a similar campaign as the need arises. In considering such additional financing, Chace/Roommaker management is looking toward MIFA for advice on marketing new bonds.

Time magazine praised the company's turnaround in its May 26, 1986, issue:

Now a $200,000 Kusters Desizing Range washes and steams raw cloth, which is then fed into a computer-controlled $1.25 million Montforts dyeing and finishing range that processes and colors 120 yards per minute, double the old rate. The firm has rehired 70% of the workers it let go last January, turning dull gray material into a rainbow of new fabrics—a metaphor for Massachusetts itself.

Chace-Roommaker needed financial help to revitalize; Ocean Spray, already an innovative company, used state assistance to expand in Southeastern Massachusetts. Its story is a remarkable tale of enterprise and initiative.

Ocean Spray packages and markets cranberry products. The cranberry is one of just three crops originally found only in North America. Harvesting and processing the cranberry is one of Massachusetts' oldest industries. So when Ocean Spray outgrew its plant in Plymouth, a state grant of $1.4 million for sewage and water helped establish a new world headquarters nearby. The development of the headquarters was a prime example of public-private cooperation in Southeastern Massachusetts; communities had to apply jointly for the grant for Ocean Spray to receive the money. CEO Hal Thorkilson called the $1.4 million the "make sense" piece that made this location "make sense" for the company's own investment of $20 million in the headquarters.

Ocean Spray Cranberries was established about sixty years ago as a cranberry growers' cooperative. The company stagnated for a long period until the mid-1970s, however, and needed to innovate to stay competitive. The cranberry business was—literally —bogged down. Then market research showed that Americans were becoming more concerned about their health and the food they ate. Since Ocean Spray drinks have on average 30 percent fruit juice, they were a logical choice. Under Hal Thorkilson's leadership, Ocean Spray began an aggressive campaign to capture a segment of the health-drink market. It began to diversify its drink line from cranberry to grapefruit, and blended juices such as Cran-Apple, nurturing its image with the advertising slogan: "It's good for you, America." Today its line includes almost a dozen drinks, including Cran-Raspberry and Cran-Blueberry.

In July 1981, the company introduced a new trademarked "paper bottle," the Brik-Pak, which helped its annual revenues jump from $361 million in fiscal 1982 to $417 million in fiscal 1983. Today the shakedown within the ready-to-serve aseptically packaged drink market has flourished, but Ocean Spray continues to hold its own. In 1983, the company appeared for the first time on the *Fortune* 500. It was number 478 in 1986 with revenues of over $600 million—and projected revenues of $1 billion by 1990.

Packaging advances such as paper bottles added to the company's healthy image and, as *Business Week* said in December 1985, "helped get its juices into the nation's lunchboxes." These paper bottles require no refrigeration and cost 15 to 20 percent less than glass.

The introduction of these Brik-Pak bottles illustrates how a smaller company can beat the corporate giants. A packaging engineer asked for and received special permission to conduct a short-term project on packaging innovation. He turned up the Brik-Paks, made by a Swedish company and a packaging technique already in use in Europe. Representatives of Tetra, the Swedish company, came to the United States to speak with representatives from several U.S. firms. One leading company was enthusiastic, so it created a task force to study the idea. Ocean Spray, on the other hand, "cut a deal within a week and obtained an eighteen-month-exclusive marketing agreement," Executive Vice President Curt Collison recalled.

Because the juice-drink market is changing rapidly, Ocean Spray is continuously experimenting with new blends, particularly with perishable fruits, new sauces, and new packaging techniques. It began selling a guava-based drink in 1985, for example, and, to keep up the pace, has recently introduced a line of aseptically packaged concentrate for its blended juices. The launching of this product, Ocean Spray Liquid Concentrate, was the company's boldest and costliest marketing scheme ever. The product, positioned to compete in the $2.9 billion frozen-concentrate market, requires no refrigeration. It also contains no artificial preservatives, because it comes in aseptic containers. Ads for the product emphasize convenience and price which, *Business Week* thinks, may be "a winning formula." The syrup—available in such flavors as Cran-Apple and Pink Grapefruit Cocktail—is 10 percent cheaper per glass than frozen concentrate and 30 percent less than bottled drinks.

Ocean Spray contributes a great deal to Southeastern Massachusetts. Because it is a cooperative, the company has a special relationship with its eight hundred growers. Collison says that the goal is "to maximize income for our suppliers, the cranberry farmers." Since packaging is such a big item for the company, relationships with other local suppliers is also very important. Furthermore, as a result of what Collison describes as a "lean and mean attitude," the company uses many consultants, working with as many as five hundred Massachusetts firms. And Ocean Spray has 1,800 full-time employees and a seasonal work force of 700 to 900.

Ocean Spray, like most innovative and successful companies, does not need a great deal of government assistance. But the Commonwealth has helped Ocean Spray wherever it could, and sometimes—as in the $1.4 million for water and sewage at the company's new headquarters—this has made a vital difference. State officials also helped Ocean Spray look at traffic patterns and mesh its plans with the state's plans for the highway near the headquarters. And the state helped Ocean Spray prepare a case for the Environmental Protection Agency in Washington to allow the use of a fungicide approved for vegetables on its cranberries.

Because of this, Ocean Spray is fully committed to expanding in Massachusetts. Collison says state government is "supportive of our company and industry," Ocean Spray is close to its source of supplies, and the area is a good place to live and work. Even though the state's prosperity means that the cost of living is high and the unskilled labor pool is shrinking, "no one wants to move." As Collison says, "We're not going to lose the momentum we've gotten from the people of this state!"

The Commonwealth's commitment to Southeastern Massachusetts investments will also make a difference for Sippican, a high-tech company with roots in the region's other traditional industry, marine equipment. If the coastal areas of Southeastern Massachusetts are to continue to live off the sea, then one way will be through advanced technology.

The U.S. Navy is locked into a naval race with the Soviets, requiring companies with whom they do business to sit on the cutting edge of technological development to make the ocean less opaque. One company whose underwater sensors and communication buoys are helping to do that job is Sippican. Though the company is a small fish in a sea of giant contractors for the U.S. Navy, chief executive Dick Arthur's goal for 1990 is to have Sippican's sales hit $100 million. A strong supporter of the Boston Celtics, he wants the company to be like Larry Bird: "big, svelte, and smooth." Like the Celtics, Sippican is well on its way to being a winner.

Sippican's headquarters, on a lovely wooded street, signals immediately the company's focus on the sea. The glass doors that separate one section of the executive office building from another are etched with fish, bubbles, and waves. The walls are covered with tasteful maritime artwork. But Sippican also participates in its region in another way: at Thanksgiving, a basket of fresh cranberries sits by the reception desk. A large spoon and brown paper bags invite employees and visitors to take a bag home.

Named after a Massachusetts Indian tribe, Sippican was formed out of the engineering consulting firm established by the father of the present chairman, Thayer "Tim" Francis. Along with William Van Clark, Jr., a former assistant dean of management at MIT, he formed the company with two other partners, whom they later bought out. The company first began to take off in 1958 when it built part of the guidance system for the navy's Polaris missile. Then in the early 1960s, the company consciously went into the field of oceanographic instrumentation because, according to Francis, "people were having a terrible time." So its first innovative product was the redesign of an antiquated, expensive bathythermograph used by the Navy to gather data on ocean temperature and currents from the surface to six thousand feet while the ship continues its course and speed.

The essential key to the innovation was understanding the market, recognizing that a ship expends more energy in stopping, and then coming back to speed, so costing more and requiring longer cruising time. From a navy standpoint, a very important extra cost was heightened vulnerability as the ship slows down. So Sippican created a new device, an expendable version called the XBT (expendable bathythermograph). The Navy was pleased with the result. It expected to pay $40 per unit, whereas Sippican's operational analysis suggested that a price of $10 would convert the market to expendable instrumentation and be a winner. In fact, that's what happened. Sippican was the first to produce the expendable variety, and this innovation allowed Sippican to corner the worldwide market for XBTs.

Since the XBT (1965), Sippican has continued to create products for deep-ocean uses requiring innovative approaches in their design and manufacture. It has developed a successful strategy of pinpointing the vulnerable products of the big companies like Raytheon, Magnavox, and Rockwell International and taking on their markets by upgrading devices, improving their reliability, or lowering their costs.

The company is now going after larger defense contracts. Its first target is a $200-million-a-year niche for sophisticated submarine detection equipment known as Vertical Line Array Difar (VLAD) sonobuoys. American Philips' Magnavox division and Spartan Corporation had split that market, but Sippican edged in on May 2, 1985, when the navy awarded it a $16 million contract to produce 7,500 VLAD sonobuoys. Using its strategy of developing a device to meet a preset cost, the company introduced a new version of the least sophisticated sonobuoy (the SSQ-36) in

1980. At a cost well below other entries, the device swept the field so that the navy now buys all its SSQ-36s from Sippican. It has recently expanded into other antisubmarine warfare markets with mine warfare and tactical communications equipment. Its most recent innovation is a product only thirty-six inches long and five inches in diameter, the Expendable Mobile Antisubmarine Warfare Training Target. This will be used for training ship and aircraft crews in operational environments.

The company is recognized within the community as a progressive, "clean" company that treats its employees well. Dick Arthur believes in "hiring brains, lots of brains." There are programs to hire the mentally and physically handicapped, as well as programs to support local colleges and civic groups. The company has developed an evening-school program in conjunction with Southeastern Massachusetts University to provide opportunities for upward mobility for its employees. The program grants a bachelor's degree either in mechanics or electrical engineering and is 100 percent reimbursable. The company is also working with Bristol Community College and MassJobs. Using facilities within Sippican as a training site, a program has been established to train assemblers in soldering electronics. Another joint venture with an educational institution is NUPRIME (Northeastern University Progress in Minority Engineering). This program identifies minority high-school students with potential in math and science, provides tutorials run at Tabor Academy, in Marion, and conducts field trips to private sector facilities. Any student who matriculates at Northeastern is awarded a scholarship by Sippican. There are presently thirty to thirty-five students enrolled in the program.

The company has always sought to apply its experience to the development of new, inexpensive expendables. The present is only different from the past in that the level of sophistication and development of products has increased. The company has made major leaps into such technologies as acoustics, hydrodynamics, and fiber optics. Dick Arthur believes that opportunities are endless for applying the company's unique experience in low-cost, high-volume manufacturing to some very sophisticated, high-tech products.

_____

Massachusetts wants companies like Sippican to keep growing in Southeastern Massachusetts. While the company is situated in a beautiful part of the state with easy access to beaches in summer and skiing in winter, it has historically been hard to attract engineers to this part of the state. That is why we are pushing the expansion of SMU and the creation of a Marine Sciences Center of Excellence.

Opportunity for All: A Regional Outlook

Even a far-reaching series of public and private investments—and a strategy that links them together—would not produce a regional economy with sustained growth, innovation, and community renewal without one other fundamental ingredient—a committed team of regional leaders who have vision, who are there for the long haul, and who are ready to submerge individual aspirations in a plan for regional progress.

When my administration came to Southeastern Massachusetts University in January of 1983, we found that the mayors of New Bedford, Fall River, and Taunton had already joined in an informal alliance for regional promotion called the Golden Triangle. Before long, the new mayors of Brockton and Attleboro had joined as well, transforming the "Golden Triangle" into the "Golden Connection." While these five cities contained most of the region's population and the alliance of their chief executives is a natural focus of leadership, other leaders were ready to do their part—area legislators, the chambers of commerce and central labor councils, the regional planning commission, SMU and the state and community colleges.

The Golden Triangle and its successor, the Golden Connection, had already embarked on a joint marketing campaign when we first met together in 1983. The first effort was a trip to Palo Alto, California, to talk to high-tech firms with the aid of a $40,000 federal grant; 120 people traveled there to sell the area, including bankers, real-estate agents, and community leaders. They prepared charts and maps, setting up their exhibit in a hotel, but not one company came to Southeastern Massachusetts.

I joined them on the next trip, this time to *Fortune* 500 companies headquartered in Connecticut. The results were again disappointing. Finally, we realized that we should stick closer to home where executives could see the area firsthand. Our state economic team compiled and contacted a list of the five hundred fastest growth companies in America, pinpointing those located in New England. The next trip became a bus tour in which New England business leaders were brought to the southeastern cities.

It did not take long for the campaign to pay off. AT&T, for example, broke ground for a $15 million office complex and data center to employ approximately a thousand people in Fairhaven, a town just across the river from New Bedford. Jon Bonsall, government relations manager for AT&T, said that "the prime reason we decided to expand in Fairhaven was that we were impressed with the positive business climate in Massachusetts, and particularly in Southeastern Massachusetts. We also encountered a lot of local support, and found a talented labor pool with a strong work ethic."

The LTX Corporation of Westwood became the first Route 128 high-tech firm to decide that labor shortages and traffic congestion on 128 could be avoided by turning to Southeastern Massachusetts for a major production expansion—bringing 200 new jobs to Fall River. Aluminum Processing Corporation of Fall River, one of the many companies that city has helped through a mixture of MIFA and UDAG financing, is expanding its job force significantly while introducing robotics into its newer process areas. Codex placed its entire 1984 expansion in production jobs—266 in all—in Bristol County; the company announced that it would continue to look south for its future in-state production growth.

By the end of 1984, the building blocks for economic development were in place in Southeastern Massachusetts. And local pride had been stimulated in many large and small ways. At the three-hundredth anniversary of Bristol County, Bob Hope came to the celebration. As Taunton Mayor Johnson said, "Five years ago we could never have gotten Bob Hope to come *here*."

But the first sign of progress is no time to rest. A 1983 report by the Bank of Boston had concluded that the combination of geography, overall economic expansion, and a decade of foundations quietly laid within Southeastern Massachusetts was finally ready to bear fruit for the region—but only if the right strategies were in place to support economic modernization. So, in October 1984, I appointed seventeen public officials and distinguished citizens to serve on SEMTECH—the Commission on Southeastern Massachusetts Technology Development. The SEMTECH membership represented an alliance of state and local government, private enterprise, organized labor, and professionals in the education and training system.

My charge to SEMTECH was to fashion a strategy for job growth in Southeastern Massachusetts that emphasized economic modernization—a set of recommendations that could help both the business community and the work force make the transition from an aging regional economy to one that could take full advantage of new technologies and new ideas.

The four strategies recommended by the SEMTECH commission in June 1985 are good illustrations of what can go into any regional development program. In this case, they required relatively little in the way of new public dollars or programs. But alongside our ongoing investments in the region's *physical plant* —its highways and downtowns and industrial parks and college campuses—these strategies for nurturing growth and change among entrepreneurs and workers have become part and parcel of our plan for Southeastern Massachusetts.

The first of the SEMTECH strategies was the creation of a fully customized and fully regional job-training capability, so that Massachusetts could offer any innovative business seeking to create or retain good jobs a publicly assisted training program tailor-made for its particular needs. With the creation of MassJobs Southeast, this challenge has been met, and companies like the brand-new Deknatel Pharmaceutical plant in Fall River know that in addition to access roads and MIFA bonds and adequate sewage treatment, Southeastern Massachusetts can provide them with custom-trained workers. In late 1987, when I helped welcome Deknatel to Fall River with its two hundred highly specialized manufacturing jobs, SEMTECH was ready.

The second SEMTECH recommendation was to make sure that the region's work force would be ready for specialized training in the first place. The region's educators have committed themselves to developing a comprehensive plan for basic technological education from the elementary-school level through the voc-tech, junior college, and bachelor's degree curricula. Because an estimated 80 percent of the year 2000 work force is already in the work force today, adult reeducation in basic technological literacy will occupy a prominent place in this overall plan.

Third, SEMTECH recommended that we plunge full-speed ahead with at least two specific ideas to nurture home-grown entrepreneurship. One is the Marine Sciences Center of Excellence, and the other is a model business incubator specializing in innovative technolgies. Through a partnership of the Massachusetts Government Land Bank and an aptly named regional non-profit development corporation called SEED, a Fall River developer, the area's first incubator is nearing construction.

Finally, SEMTECH reminded us that teamwork and regional marketing are essential elements in any plan to persuade outside decision makers that Southeastern Massachusetts can be a hotbed of innovation and economic change.

In 1987, that outlook reached new heights when the five Golden Connection mayors joined the president of SMU to form the Southeastern Massachusetts Partnership. Brenda Reed, the former mayor of Attleboro who brought that city into the Golden Connection and served on the SEMTECH Commission, is now my development coordinator for Southeastern Massachusetts. She points out that "the university is the anchor . . . because the rest of us come and go but this partnership has to stay and grow." The new partnership will be a central resource of academic strength, regional unity, and political support for all of the other development enterprises underway or planned.

The first $100,000 in center funding came from the state government in 1987, along with $10,000 from each of the five cities. Because of this partnership, the Bank of Boston pledged $2.5 million in low-interest loans for business expansion as well as the invaluable ongoing alliance of one of New England's premier financial institutions.

What's happening in Southeastern Massachusetts is unique in the sense that the public strategy is tailored to the assets and aspirations of this particular area. But it is certainly not unique in the applicability of such an approach to any economically deprived region that has good people and the dream of opportunity. In Massachusetts alone, we are engaged in very similar partnerships with northern Berkshire County, the Northern Tier of Franklin and Worcester Counties, and a wonderful area rich in history and potential called the Blackstone Valley. In all of these areas, unemployment has dropped dramatically and the roots of a sustained regional comeback are taking hold.

Every regional strategy is a blend of the elements that have begun to work effectively in Southeastern Massachusetts: business expansion keyed by innovative entrepreneurship; rebuilt communities whose downtowns and neighborhoods link economic growth to the people who need it; and education and training programs that reflect the needs of the 1980s and 1990s. Environmental protection and the quality of life play a key role in each instance, for tourists, longtime residents, and newcomers alike.

In no instance has Massachusetts tried to rebuild a regional economy from the top down. Rather, we have joined hands with the people of each region to call forth *their* leadership and *their* creativity. It is an approach that works in Massachusetts—and can work across America.

CHAPTER SIX

Innovation and Opportunity: The Next American Frontier

There is a lesson for America in the Massachusetts success story. It is not that every specific program we tried here will work everywhere else. Rather, the lesson is in the *idea* of hands-on economic development and the *approach* we've used to get it done.

We got our fiscal house in order.

We *invested* in public infrastructure, worker training, and capital formation—and got the private sector to invest much more.

We set our sights on the two fundamental goals of a bright and just economic future—*innovation* and *opportunity*.

We understood that economic development happens not in abstract statistics, but in real *places*, through the hard work of real *people*.

And we found our greatest success in the creation of *partnerships*—grass-roots alliances of business, labor, community leaders, and educators, supported and encouraged by state government but rooted in the wisdom and dedication of others.

Massachusetts is hardly alone. In state after state, creative governors and legislatures are working with *their* business and labor leaders, *their* mayors and county commissioners and college presidents, to forge partnerships that make a difference in the lives and well-being of people and communities. It is from the state houses of America, and not the White House, that economic leadership has come these past seven years.

And there is a lesson in that leadership. It is that a true strategy for national economic recovery must reach into America's shop floors and research labs, her schools and training centers, her downtowns and neighborhoods. And most important of all, a truly national economic strategy must reach into every region of every state in this land.

As important as sound macroeconomic policies are, they are merely the foundations on which innovation and opportunity must be built. We need something more. A flourishing of innovation and opportunity across America will require Washington to reach out, to call forth an awakening of state, local, and regional partnerships, and to support them not only with dollars, but with attention and a sense of urgency. In short, we need our national government to join up, to assume its indispensable role in a *national partnership* for economic recovery.

Getting the Nation's Fiscal House in Order

That partnership won't get off the ground if America's economy continues to choke on an annual budget deficit of $150 to $200 billion. According to the Commerce Department, "the critical element [in producing our trade imbalance] was the expansion of the federal budget deficit from about $60 billion in 1980 to over $200 billion in 1985." The debt service that carries that deficit not only drives up interest rates and depletes American savings, but balloons the deficit even more, sapping the national government's ability to invest in the makings of innovation and growth.

Without those record-high deficits, American savings would have been enough to meet America's public and private investment needs. The value of the dollar would not have skyrocketed. A massive influx of foreign capital would not have occurred. America would not have become a debtor nation. And our huge trade deficit would be far, far smaller than it is today.

There are only four ways to reduce the budget deficit: control spending, improve our economic performance, bring down interest rates, and increase federal revenues. And they must be done simultaneously.

We cannot afford and we don't need Star Wars and $18 billion Supercarrier task forces and $50 billion worth of Midgetman missiles.

We can save billions more on the domestic side of the budget by helping hundreds of thousands of families to get off welfare, encouraging senior citizens to enroll in quality prepaid health plans, limiting federal farm subsidies to small- and medium-sized family farms, and eliminating spending on a three-hour space plane from Washington to Tokyo.

We can cut billions more off the deficit by getting our rate of economic growth up and by bringing interest rates down. If we had 4 percent unemployment today instead of 6, the federal budget deficit would be *seventy billion dollars less*. And every percentage point reduction in interest reduces the federal deficit by *another fifteen billion dollars*.

We also need more revenue. And the best and fairest way to get it is by enforcing federal tax laws. According to the Internal Revenue Service, tax compliance at the federal level has dropped to 81 percent. That represents over $100 billion in federal taxes that go uncollected every year—over half the federal deficit. Left unchecked this tax gap will hit $200 billion by the early 1990s.

A bipartisan task force on federal revenue enforcement,

chaired by Congressman Byron Dorgan, has estimated that by raising tax compliance five percentage points we could increase revenues by $35 billion a year. Not to do that is more than dumb fiscal policy. It's simply not fair to the overwhelming majority of Americans who pay their taxes in full and on time.

The REAP program in Massachusetts—the Revenue Enforcement and Protection effort that I described in chapter 1—began in 1983 with the first budget I submitted after being returned to office. It has exceeded every expectation for revenue yield while assuring the average taxpaying citizen of the Commonwealth that everyone is contributing his or her fair share to the economic investments we have made during these past five years.

Does tough revenue enforcement work only in heavily urban or industrial states? Kent Conrad, the revenue commissioner of North Dakota, challenged the skeptics and designed a revenue enforcement plan that generated a return on investment of 1,400 percent!

In fact eighteen states—states with Republican as well as Democratic governors, states as different as Massachusetts, Illinois, New York, California, and North Dakota—have used aggressive and creative tax compliance programs to help get their fiscal houses in order. How on earth can Washington turn its back on a federal opportunity of even greater dimensions?

Of course, no responsible candidate for the presidency can rule out the possibility of new taxes. But that's a question we can't answer until we know how much revenue a tax compliance program can raise and how much we need.

Education and Infrastructure:
The Essential Public Investments

None of our ideas for economic recovery and growth, none of the partnerships we need to build, will go very far without most fundamental ingredients. One is a well-educated and well-trained citizenry—literate and confident and ready to tackle the demands of a changing economy. The other is the bricks and mortar and steel and asphalt of a modern economic infrastructure. To treat either of these requirements as anything less than a top national priority is as penny-wise and pound-foolish a choice as America could ever make.

Four years ago America was riveted by the findings of a national report that found we were a nation at risk in a rising tide of educational mediocrity. Much has been done by *the states* since then.

The Carnegie Commission reports that we have made "a good beginning in the search for an educational renaissance in America," and I can tell you that this renaissance has its roots in the vision of state governments. In the words of New Jersey Governor Tom Kean, chairman of the National Governors' Association Task Force on Education, "What Governors are doing for the schools is a compelling expression of faith in the future of this country." But we still have much to do:

- test scores lagging behind the Japanese and the West Germans;
- 7,700 American high schools without a single course in physics because they have no one qualified to teach it;
- a quarter of our public school students dropping out before finishing high school;
- the highest rate of drug abuse in any Western nation in our schools;
- twenty-five million Americans unable to read;
- too many youngsters cutting short their education.

Now it's time for a *national* partnership for educational excellence—one in which the president becomes this nation's number one advocate for good teaching and good schools. We'll have to begin by focusing on the most important educational priorities. Let me suggest three.

First and most important is *teaching*. Over the next decade, *half our public school teachers will retire from teaching,* and their replacements are nowhere in sight. We already have 35,000 teaching vacancies across the country and severe shortages in science, math, and foreign languages. America needs a national teaching excellence fund—a first-year investment of a quarter billion dollars in a venture capital fund for good teaching.

We need scholarships for young people willing to make a commitment to teaching after they graduate. We need a revived national teacher corps—a domestic Peace Corps for teaching, and we need sabbaticals, opportunities for veteran teachers to be at field centers of teaching and learning—to revive and refresh and improve their knowledge and skills.

A second focus must be the eradication of adult illiteracy. This is a priority for the National Governors' Association, and good state programs—emphasizing public, private, and volunteer commitments—can be found all across America. I've proposed an annual $25 million federal challenge to the private sector—an amount which, when matched by the business community, will provide seed grants to expand state and local literacy programs.

The third priority in our national partnership for educational excellence is college opportunity. No youngster who graduates from high school and is admitted to college should ever be denied that opportunity because of financial need. The annual assault on Pell grants and student loans must stop. *But we can do more.* Every state could create a college opportunity fund—a way for families to prepay their children's tuition, at guaranteed rates, at the college of their choice. Most state colleges and universities should adopt a policy of tuition waivers based on financial need.

Furthermore, I believe we can create a national educational insurance program through which those who need tuition assistance would draw benefits from a trust fund and then replenish it through income withholding—a kind of educational social security system in reverse.

Unlike education, public infrastructure is an area in which

we do not need innovative new programs. We know what has to be done—if we want a first-rate transportation system and clean air and clean water. What we need is an end to the fiscal myopia that has enabled the president to brand the rebuilding of our economic lifelines as "wasteful spending." How misguided is that view?

Greater Boston is a world center of finance, technology, education, medicine, and communications. It is a labor market of some two million workers, the economic center of New England, a major exporter of America's most innovative products, and a global destination for travelers. Without improved highways and public transit, the region's movement of goods and services will grind to a crawl. Without the cleanup of Boston Harbor, the law of the land will require a halt to new sewer hookups. Either way, economic growth would stop, and that would clearly be bad for the economy. Other states and cities face similar challenges.

Yet in early 1987, both the Highway Bill and the Clean Water Act—the funding sources for these essential projects—had to be passed by Congress over President Reagan's veto. What kind of economic strategy is that?

In every region of the country, economic recovery and expansion depend on good transportation and improved environmental quality. Most needed infrastructure projects are less visible and expensive than Greater Boston's two "megaprojects." But ask yourself how many plant expansions or downtown office buildings or neighborhood housing renovations are built where highway access is inadequate, or streets and sidewalks and playgrounds are disaster areas, or nearby ports and rail sidings are crumbling, or every square foot of new development adds to the pollution of a river, or there is no place to park?

Several federal grant programs assist states and localities with these critical needs. To be sure, not every project is essential and some may be unwise. But national leadership that understands economic development must work closely with governors and local officials to identify the priorities and get them built.

Delay doesn't make roads and sewers and transit systems any less important—it just makes them cost more.

A Partnership with America's Innovators

More than at any other time in this century, Americans are preoccupied with the competitive stance of this nation's economy in the much larger economy of the world. As American industries lose market share to overseas rivals, American workers lose good jobs and American communities suffer the effects of dislocation and disinvestment.

But too much of what is usually said about international competitiveness misses the point because we tend to divide every speaker and every proposal into two camps—protectionist and free trade. But what do those labels mean?

Is it protectionist when Massachusetts helps a textile company like Chace/Roommaker to modernize its equipment and upgrade the skills of its work force to compete in a world market? Or when we promote photovoltaic cell technology and invest in ventures like Spire and Kopin? Or when we help Ocean Spray absorb the costs of new water and sewer lines so that a larger and more technologically advanced world headquarters can pump out more soft-pack fruit juices?

Not long ago I met with the economic minister of the West German state of Baden-Württemberg, where industry-university partnerships assisted by government have retooled and saved the textile industry. When I asked him how long this sort of joint enterprise had been going on, he said, "Since Bismarck."

What about us? What kind of reputation will the label "Made in U.S.A." have in the world five or ten years from now? How do we dispense with the myth that America must inevitably deindustrialize, that we can provide services *to* others but must buy products *from* others?

The time to begin is now. In 1987 the trade deficit was a record $175 billion, up from a record $156 billion in 1986. Farm exports have declined by 37 percent in six years, and more than a million manufacturing jobs have been lost during the same period.

The plea for a level playing field on which to compete economically is a just and fair plea. And it may be necessary at times to impose some barriers to trade—but only if those barriers are limited in time and require the beneficiary to invest and modernize and become competitive.

In 1983, competition from imports was driving Harley-Davidson, America's last producer of motorcycles, out of business. The company sought and received temporary tariff protection. But that protection was limited to five years and it was provided only because of Harley's concrete plan to modernize. Harley did modernize—it introduced new manufacturing practices, improved product design, and raised the percentage of motorcycles leaving the assembly line without defects from 50 percent to 98 percent.

In 1987, Harley-Davidson went to Washington with a new request—to get rid of those tariffs. The company is now competing in an open market. I visited Harley-Davidson's plant in Milwaukee, and I saw an American factory where management and labor are working together and are succeeding together.

But even temporary and carefully targeted restrictions on imports like these should be the exception and not the rule. Unfair trade practices are only a partial cause of our trade deficit, and a trade war—like any war—will produce only victims, not victors. If every trade barrier to American goods disappeared tomorrow, we would still have a trade deficit in excess of $100 billion.

We must act. Bringing down our crippling federal budget deficit is essential. But so is a simple and obvious truth—to compete, we must be competitive. And competitiveness requires innovation, in new and mature industries alike.

Today, Japan invests three times as much in manufacturing technology as we do. The Japanese invest more in new plants and equipment; they invest more in civilian research. They graduate 50 percent more scientists, mathematicians, and engineers, and their entire educational system is geared, with public leadership and support, toward economic growth and success in the world market.

In recent years, I twice joined with elected officials from across America to shape new initiatives for economic competitiveness—first as chairman of the Committee on the Industrial and Entrepreneurial Economy of the Democratic Policy Commission, and then as cochair of the National Governors' Association Task Force on Jobs, Growth, and Competitiveness.

And I learned that whereas other nations devote as much as 14 percent of their government research budgets to advance industrial growth, the United States is at 1 percent. We simply must recognize that research and development for our economic future are every bit as important as weapons research— and we must act accordingly.

The research-and-development tax credit must become a permanent feature of the federal tax code, so that innovative entrepreneurs across this land have the incentive they need to try new ideas.

America needs a national network of Centers of Excellence to foster innovation at the cutting edge of science and technology. These centers would be the laboratories for the American economy of the future, greenhouses where business and education would join forces in cooperative research and development, both basic and applied.

Moreover, by linking these centers to the special strengths of the nation's regional economies, we can help restore economic health to distressed areas. Under the leadership of Governor Jim Blanchard, Michigan is working hard to make the automobile industry and its suppliers a center of manufacturing excellence. That's more than a Michigan priority; it's an American priority, and Michigan's program should be elevated to a national center of manufacturing excellence with ample federal support.

In the Pacific Northwest, where the timber industry and its workers are suffering through a deep depression and cutthroat foreign competition, a Center of Excellence could explore ways in which new technology could create whole new uses for wood products or vastly reduce the cost of home building, thereby increasing demand for timber products.

Hard-hit American farmers could benefit from a Center of Excellence designed to promote food-related biotechnology, create exciting new uses for our crops, like ethanol and biodegradable plastics, discover new markets, cut costs through reduced use of pesticides, and add value by developing new food products from our basic crops. Thanks to Senator Tom Harkin and Congressman Neal Smith, Iowa State University will soon be the site of just such a Center of Excellence.

America has done this before. Our country's preeminent position in agriculture grew out of the long-standing partnership between the Department of Agriculture, our land-grant universities, and the nation's farmers, eager to experiment with new crops and new farming techniques and technologies. America's initial lead in electronics was spawned by the teamwork of universities, individual entrepreneurs, government, and venture capitalists, all lending their skills to creating an entire new industry.

Until recently, only the states were experimenting with partnerships for new technologies. In response to the growing Japanese ascendancy in computer chips, Texas, North Carolina, and Massachusetts have created microelectronics centers of world caliber.

Pennsylvania's Ben Franklin Partnership, perhaps the nation's most ambitious state technology development program, combines cooperative R & D funding, venture capital, and full-service incubators at four university centers in different parts of the state.

And then there is New York. In 1978, then Governor Hugh Carey planted an important research-and-development seed. Seeking a solution to the economic problems that were afflicting the community of Troy—which once flourished as the home of the Bessemer steel process—Governor Carey proposed the drafting of a state high-tech policy. An immediate by-product of this policy was a proposal to fund a $30 million integrated electronics building at Rensselaer Polytechnic Institute in Troy.

Then, under Governor Mario Cuomo, this initial seed blossomed into full flower—seven Centers for Advanced Technology located at seven universities around the state, each funded at $1 million for four years. These state dollars must be matched by industry contributions. They are supporting research in computer and information systems, biotechnology for agriculture, telecommunications, health-care instruments and devices, medical biotechnology, advanced optical technology, and computer applications and software engineering.

The approach of states like New York, Pennsylvania, and Massachusetts shows how the promotion of strategic technologies can be combined with the revitalization of regional economies. That is the model for a federal initiative. National Centers of Excellence can be created through federal support of existing state technology centers, or through the pooling of public and private and university resources to form entirely new centers.

In the last two years, the National Science Foundation has begun to organize its Science Engineering Centers, eleven of which are now operating. In a separate development, SEMA-TECH—a $1.25 billion, nationwide public-private R & D consortium designed to recapture world microelectronics leadership for the United States—will soon set up shop in Austin, Texas. It is time to recognize in these fledgling national efforts a truly powerful idea and a true key to America's economic future.

A Partnership with America's Communities

Innovation and opportunity meet in the cities and towns of America. And the reverse is true as well. Communities that are falling apart have a hard time attracting risk-taking entrepreneurs who need good infrastructure, stable municipal services, a respectable business address, neighborhoods that are good neighbors, and a qualified work force. At the same time, communities that lack those fundamental strengths cannot translate their economic assets that do attract into genuine opportunity for their people.

That is why America must reach out to cities and towns large and small, urban and rural, to *encourage* public-private partnerships for community revitalization, and to *support* them. Massachusetts and many other states have done just that—but we need the recognition that healthy, optimistic, and economically sound communities are at the heart of any national economic strategy.

Fortunately, some important community development programs have survived the wrecking ball of the past seven years. Community development block grants enable cities and towns to keep their basic infrastructure in shape, to maintain their housing stock, to make progress on the nation's Main Streets and municipal industrial parks, and to fund some basic human resource programs.

Urban development action grants enable communities to reach beyond their ongoing revitalization programs to land the occasional "big one"—an industrial, residential, or commercial development that will have a major impact on the local economy. These bread-and-butter programs are very important.

But there is one area in which national policy is lagging way behind local initiative, and American communities are suffering as a result. And that is the area of decent and affordable housing.

The National Housing Act of 1949 was cosponsored by a conservative Republican, Senator Robert Taft of Ohio, and it established bipartisan support for the principle of decent housing for all Americans. That bipartisan support continued through every postwar administration—Republican as well as Democratic—until the Reagan years. Under both Presidents Ford and Carter, America was building or rehabilitating more than 200,000 units of housing for individuals and families of low and moderate income every year. But during the past seven years, we have walked away from our commitment to decent and affordable housing for all our people. No wonder there are thousands of families and individuals sleeping on the streets and in the doorways of American cities. No wonder we have to apologize to foreign visitors who ask how it is that the most affluent nation on the face of the earth can tolerate this shameful spectacle of hundreds of thousands of American citizens without a roof over their heads.

State and local housing partnerships across the country, including the ones we have developed in Massachusetts, have shown the way that the housing crisis can be solved. These partnerships come in many varieties:

- In Cleveland, millions of dollars in corporate bonds are going into neighborhood housing.
- In New York, the ironworkers are using their pension funds to finance reduced-rate mortgages.
- In San Francisco, the Bridge Housing Corporation is building thousands of units of housing through public-private cooperation.
- In Chattanooga, a new partnership has set for itself the goal of guaranteeing a decent and affordable home or apartment for every resident of the city.
- In Boston, the bricklayers' union has formed a nonprofit housing subsidiary that pays its workers full union scale and, with help from both city and state governments, is building new housing young families can buy at a third less than the going market rate.

On a statewide basis, our own Massachusetts Housing Partnership, which I described in detail in chapter 3, is showing the way. The Massachusetts initiative is building three different kinds of new and rehabilitated housing—small, scattered-site public housing; mixed-income private rental housing; and affordable housing for ownership. Massachusetts is focusing special attention on one of the most acute housing issues facing older cities—the problem of abandonment—as well as the land-use and growth-management issues facing more affluent, growing communities.

Most important of all, we are not trying to do all this through an overly centralized state bureaucracy that pretends to know what is best in every Massachusetts community. Rather, the Massachusetts Housing Partnership is a statewide mobilization of local partnerships—public-private collaborations that need and get the state's technical assistance and financial support.

That is what I have in mind when I travel across this country and call for a *National Partnership for Affordable Housing*. We don't need a massive new federal construction program that repeats old mistakes. We need a creative alliance of state and local partnerships supported by federal leadership that cares. We need presidential and congressional leadership to bring together everyone in this country who cares about decent, affordable housing and can do something about it—governors and legislatures, mayors and city councils, county commissioners, developers, building-trade unions, bankers, housing advocates, and community-action agencies.

A National Partnership for Affordable Housing should work aggressively to achieve three common goals:

- to build and rehabilitate good housing at affordable prices;
- to protect our existing investment in low- and moderate-income housing from expiring contract restrictions and wholesale disinvestment;
- to expand homeownership opportunities for young families and other first-time buyers who, for the first time since World War II, are finding the American dream of owning a house beyond their reach.

In December of 1987, the Congress approved the first housing legislation in six years. In addition to reauthorizing some important housing and community development programs, this bill takes some steps toward protecting existing affordable housing and encouraging state and local partnerships like the ones I have described.

It will be the job of the next president to lead the Congress toward a full-scale National Partnership for Affordable Housing. We know that decent, affordable housing is an indispensable part of the fabric of American communities. And we know that only in strong communities can economic innovation and economic opportunity flourish.

H. L. Mencken, who lived in the same house in Baltimore for forty-five years, one said:

> A home is not a mere transient shelter; its essence lies . . . in its quality of representing, in all its details, the personalities of the people who live in it . . . they give it its indefinable air, separating it from all other homes, as one human face is separated from all others.

As America faces the twenty-first century, we must say the same for her neighborhoods and her communities.

A Partnership with America's Workers

We have already identified education, from kindergarten through college, as an obvious and irreplaceable ingredient of America's economic future. But there is a further need, the need to link American workers—and Americans who want to be workers—with the jobs our economy produces. That challenge is becoming more complex every day.

- Between now and the year 2000, literally millions of jobs in manufacturing and traditional service industries will change radically or become obsolete.

- The new jobs coming on-line will require ever-higher skill levels from a year 2000 work force, some 80 percent of which is already working today.
- Smaller companies, which produce most new jobs and most of our innovations, find it hardest to provide training on their own.
- Nearly fourteen million young Americans are growing up in poverty, with dependency rather than work as a model for later life.

In the face of these challenges, the nation's principal employment and training program—the Job Training Partnership Act —needs to be strengthened, deepened, and broadened, not cut repeatedly.

JTPA is a good model. It revolves around area partnerships rather than centralized bureaucracy; it reaches out to key populations like disadvantaged youth and dislocated workers; it responds to the needs of regional economies; and it has encouraged the beginnings of genuine collaboration among the states' training systems, employment services, and vocational schools.

Yet JTPA must do more, and I propose a better and stronger Job Training Partnership that does three things. First, the national effort to retrain and reemploy workers whose jobs have fallen victim to technological change must increase. In 1987, the Congress considered a worker adjustment bill that would have provided hundreds of millions of dollars in additional training and placement funds for dislocated workers paid for with a very modest one-half of one percent fee on goods imported into the United States.

I'm for that kind of program. America can't afford to tell its blue-collar work force that when a plant closes or a process line changes, it's the end of the trail. At the Quincy Shipyard in Massachusetts and the San Jose auto assembly plant in California, well-planned and caring reemployment programs found decent jobs for most of the victims of two massive closings. These are models for national action. By helping the hundreds of thousands of experienced American workers each year who are caught in the winds of change, we can advance the progress of innovation *and* keep the promise of opportunity.

A thoughtful dislocated worker program should also work to *prevent* dislocation. Companies that are planning to modernize their production lines should receive every encouragement to upgrade the skills of their existing work force. In conjunction with new Centers of Excellence in applied manufacturing technology, a well-funded and flexible dislocated-worker program should operate at the heart of a strengthened Job Training Partnership.

Second, a strengthened jobs partnership demands national welfare reform. The nation's governors have urged the Congress to enact a national program patterned on the experience of Massachusetts and a growing number of other states.

The Congress must make sure that JTPA resources are adequate to support welfare-to-work programs in all the states, and that Aid to Families with Dependent Children, our principal welfare program, provides a federal match for state investments in child care, transportation, and health insurance for welfare recipients who are taking the vital transitional step into the world of work.

Third, the Congress should create the strongest link possible between state job training systems and state employment services. In particular, I believe we should allow states that enjoy large balances in their unemployment insurance trust funds to use a small percentage of that balance to support customized training programs for workers and their employers.

Whether the special economic challenge is upgrading the skills of auto-part makers in Michigan, bringing neighborhood youth into the booming construction industry of Greater Boston, or training workers to master office automation in downtown business districts all over America, states need the flexibility to develop employment and training programs that provide good customized training for skills that are in increasingly short supply in many parts of the country.

A Partnership for All America

I am proud to be governor of a state that in 1987 had an unemployment rate of 3.2 percent, where the personal income of its citizens continues to grow, whose economy generated some 60,000 new jobs last year, whose businesses are ready to take risks and whose people are closer than ever to the dream of genuine opportunity for all. And I'm proud to have had something to do with my state's economic resurgence.

But what Massachusetts faced twelve years ago is all too suggestive of what America faces today. In 1987, too many states were still in recession, and even in generally prosperous states we still find regions, both metropolitan and rural, in deep economic trouble.

In the fall of 1987, I went to the Iron Range of Minnesota, where 10,000 jobs have been lost in the previous eight years; to Waterloo, Iowa, where 13,000 jobs were lost in seven years; and to the Rio Grande Valley of Texas, where some counties have unemployment rates of 20 and 25 and 30 percent.

Situations like these are simply unacceptable if we are serious about America's economic future and its people. But change will not happen by accident. Innovation and opportunity did not simply trickle into Southeastern Massachusetts, and they will not simply trickle into the distressed regions I have visited in my campaign for the presidency. Just as Massachusetts has helped to rebuild her Targets for Opportunity, America must help her state and local leaders build sustained economic recovery in every region of every state.

One way to do that is to make existing economic development programs work better. I've already discussed important infrastructure and capital formation programs like community development block grants and urban development action grants. There are others as well, like the small business and industrial development efforts in the Commerce Department. And as I've stated repeatedly, our basic regional infrastructure is as critical to economic growth as it is to safe transportation and a clean environment.

A fresh look at any or all of these programs might yield a biggger bang for the buck through better organization or greater productivity, and I'm for that. But even more important is the need to cut through the fragmentation and lack of regional focus that so often characterize the implementation of federal development programs. A small federal team of regional specialists, working with governors, mayors, and county officials to fashion individual projects into coordinated regional agendas, could make a real difference.

That kind of coordination will be particularly important if the *new* partnership initiatives I have called for are to be folded into regional development strategies. A National Partnership for Affordable Housing, a strengthened Job Training Partnership, and a national Centers of Excellence network—these initiatives are important not only because affordable housing, good training, and new technologies are valuable in their own right, but because they are part and parcel of what every region needs to shape a bright economic future.

For all these reasons, I believe we need a new centerpiece for developing and implementing regional economic strategies— the *Fund to Rebuild America*. The fund would be financed at an annual level of $500 million—not in place of other development programs, but alongside them, to provide special help to communities and regions that are hurting badly. Five hundred million dollars is just one-tenth of what the Reagan administration wanted to spend on Star Wars in 1987, but what a difference it could make.

The fund would make good on America's need to reinvest in its economically troubled regions. The investments would be in familiar areas—infrastructure, capital, and job training. But *these* investments would be special.

First and foremost, they would have to reflect a true *public-private partnership* at the grass roots. As we have proven time and again in Massachusetts, regional economic development works best when it springs from the vision of local officials, business people, labor leaders, community groups, and educators. State and federal allies—no matter how much they care—simply cannot hope to substitute their own prescriptions for the shared wisdom of those who live in, work in, and lead the region. The Fund to Rebuild America should not only look to the priorities set by regional partnerships, but should provide financial support for their creation and staffing.

Second, the fund should get involved in a regional development only if the *state government* in question is actively involved as well. For that is another obvious lesson from what states like Michigan, New York, North Carolina, Pennsylvania, and Massachusetts have achieved in the last decade. States control much of the flow of federal dollars in areas like infrastructure and job training, and creative state governments can fashion strategic reinvestment programs of their own that make sense for their communities, industries, and regions. Their participation is essential.

Third, the fund should assist those economic investments that are *truly strategic*—centerpiece initiatives that are unlikely to be made adequately, with sufficient coordination, and on time through regular programs. What did the Lowell Urban Heritage State Park and the revitalization of the entire central city mean to the growth of the Merrimack Valley? What did the Myles Standish Industrial Park mean to the renewal and diversification of manufacturing in Southeastern Massachusetts? What might expanding businesses mean to the Rio Grande Valley, or the revitalization of the Mississippi riverfront to Greater Dubuque, or the creation of business incubators on the Iron Range?

These efforts, and dozens like them, don't fall neatly into our investment categories of infrastructure, capital, and training. Nor are they restricted to a single kind of development—industrial, commercial, or residential. With the help of a federal development team that reaches out and listens, regional priorities like these would receive assistance from regular development programs as well as the Fund to Rebuild America. But the fund would be the glue that holds the key strategic initiatives together.

Fourth, the fund should be *targeted*. Unlike most federal programs, the fund should allocate its resources on a competitive basis rather than through a formula. And the competition should be directed very specifically to regions that are in economic distress. Most of the fund's dollars should go to states with high unemployment, fiscal troubles, and serious regional problems; fund dollars that go to more fortunate states must be restricted to regions with lagging economies and a clear need for help.

Conclusion

My vision of America's economic future is one in which the spirit of innovation lives and moves in every corner of this land, and every citizen enjoys genuine economic opportunity. And I believe that it is a fundamental duty of our national government to help bring that vision to life.

America needs more than traditional economic policies. America needs to invest in the nuts, bolts, and brains of economic growth. We must fashion those investments into a web of partnerships that reach into America's industries and communities. And we must make sure that growing and durable regional economies—with good jobs, good wages, and hope for the future—take root everywhere.

Why should we do these things? Certainly not out of charity, and not even because it's right or fair. But because we are one country, and when farms are foreclosed in Iowa or South Dakota, the plant in Illinois that makes the tractor, the mill in Pittsburgh that supplies the steel, the refinery in Texas that fuels the forge, and the software company in New England that ensures quality in the steel plant all hang in the balance.

The real question we face, not just in 1988 but for the rest of this century, is: do we have the will, the strength, and the determination to build that web of partnerships, to make those important investments, to stick with the job until the job is done?

It's time we recalled the vision upon which this nation was founded two centuries ago. After all, what was it that brought representatives from the thirteen colonies to Philadelphia that hot summer? They had won their freedom; but their first effort at self-government, under the Articles of Confederation, had gone astray.

The reason was clear—each colony had tried to go it alone. There were thirteen separate states, thirteen systems of commerce and currency, thirteen strategies for economic and military security, thirteen visions of the future. It couldn't work.

And so the farmers of Virginia, the merchants of Massachusetts, and the artisans of New York joined their futures and their destinies in a new system. And their vision—of states and regions working together—made this country the strongest nation on earth.

It is that timeless connection between national prosperity and the well-being of each family and community, between the wellspring of American ingenuity and the contribution of individual entrepreneurs and workers, that we must rediscover. And by doing so we will create in the next American frontier a nation in which there is *genuine* opportunity for every single citizen— rich or poor, young or old, black or brown, yellow or white.

Bibliography

ADY, ROBERT M. 1983. "High-Technology Plants—Different Criteria for the Best Location." *Commentary* (Winter): 8–10.

———. 1981. "Shifting Factors in Plant Location." *Industrial Development* 150 (November–December): 13–17.

BARBER, PETE J. 1982. "The Site Selection Process at Honeywell." *Industrial Development* 151 (November–December): 9–11.

BARONE, MICHAEL. 1986. "Poor Children and Politics." *The Washington Post* (February 10), p. A 11.

The Bay State Skills Corporation: 1981–1986 Evolution and Innovation. 1987. Report of the Bay State Skills Corporation. Boston, MA.

BELLIN, JEFFREY DAVID. 1981. *The Funding, Growth, and Development of Technically Based Enterprises.* Cambridge, MA: MIT Sloan School, unpublished Master's thesis.

BERMAN, NORTON L. n.d. "Trends in Economic Development—Meanings for the Sun Belt." In The Fantus Company Management Report.

BIRCH, DAVID L. 1981a. *Choosing a Place to Grow; Business Location Decisions in the 1970's.* Cambridge, MA: MIT Program on Neighborhood and Regional Change.

————. 1981b. "Who Creates Jobs?" *The Public Interest* 65 (Fall): 3–14

————. 1979. *The Job Generation Process.* Cambridge, MA; MIT Program on Neighborhood and Regional Change.

BISCOMB, RICHARD L. 1980. "The Availability and Cost of Personnel as a Factor in the Location Decision." *Industrial Development* 159 (March–April): 20–25.

BLUESTONE, BARRY AND BENNETT HARRISON. 1982. *The Deindustrialization of America.* New York: Basic Books.

BLUMENTHAL, ADAM. 1986. "Revitalization Through Partnership." Cambridge, MA: John F. Kennedy School of Government, Harvard University, Center for Business and Government.

BOLTON, ROGER. 1980. "Impacts of Defense Spending on Urban Areas." In *The Urban Impacts of Federal Policies*, Norman J. Glickman (ed.), Baltimore: The Johns Hopkins University Press: pp. 151–174.

BOTKIN, JAMES, DAN DIMANCESCU, AND RAY STATA. 1984. *The Innovators: Rediscovering America's Creative Energy.* New York: Harper and Row.

BRODER, DAVID S. 1986. "New Deal-Making Politics: Massachusetts Governor Develops a Machine." *The Washington Post* (February 10).

BRODY, HERB. 1985. "States Vie for a Slice of the Pie." *High Technology* (January): 16–28.

BROOKS, GERALDINE. 1985. "The Road Back: Old New England City Heals Itself." *The Wall Street Journal* (February 1).

BROWNE, LYNNE E. 1981. "A Quality Labor Supply." *New England Economic Review* (July–August): 19–36.

CARLTON, DENNIS W. 1979. "Why New Firms Locate Where They Do: An Econometric Model." In William C. Wheaton (ed.), *Interregional Movements and Regional Growth.* Washington, D.C.: The Urban Institute: pp. 13–50.

"Centers for Excellence." 1986. Report of the Executive Office of Economic Affairs. Boston, MA.

"The Checklist of Expansion Planning and Site Selection Factors." 1979. *Site Selection Handbook*: pp. 12–31.

Coakly, Michael. 1985. "Jewel Glistens in Rust Belt." *Chicago Tribune* (March 10): Section 1, p. 8.

Commonwealth of Massachusetts. 1986. *The Governor's Training and Employment Plan: Program Years 1986–1987.* (May 15).

COOPER, ARNOLD C. 1975. "Incubator Organizations and Other Influences on Entrepreneurship." In Shreier, *et al, Entrepreneurship and Enterprise Development: A World-Wide Perspective.* Milwaukee: The Center for Venture Management: pp. 529–532

———. 1972. "Incubator Organizations and Technical Entrepreneurship." In Cooper and Komives, *Technical Entrepreneurship: A Symposium.* Milwaukee: The Center for Venture Management: pp. 108–125.

——— and John L. Komives (eds.). 1972. *Technical Entrepreneurship: A Symposium.* Milwaukee: The Center for Venture Management.

Creating the Future: Economic Innovation for the Twenty-First Century. 1986. The Report of the Governor's Advisory Committee on Innovation. Commonwealth of Massachusetts (October).

DAVIDSON, JOE. 1986. "More States Now Ask Recipients of Aid to Train and Take Jobs." *The Wall Street Journal* (July 23): 1 +.

DORFMAN, NANCY S. 1982. *Massachusetts' High-Technology Boom in Perspective: An Investigation of Its Dimensions, Causes, and of the Role of New Firms.* Cambridge, MA: Center For Policy Alternatives, MIT (April) CPA 82–2.

"Dukakis Counts His Accomplishments." 1986. Interview in *Mass High Tech* (December 16–January 5): 13 +.

DUKAKIS, MICHAEL S. 1985. "TARGETS FOR OPPORTUNITY." REMARKS, BOSTON, MA (JANUARY 19).

———. 1986. "Massachusetts: Creating the Future—Today." State of the State Address. Delivered before both Houses of the General Court of Massachusetts (January 14).

————. 1986. "For a Tax Amnesty to Cut the Deficit." *The New York Times* (February 26).

————. 1986. "Tax Amnesty Is Not Unfair." *The Washington Post* (March 15).

————. 1986. Interview in *Impact*.

————. 1986. "Creating the Future: Teamwork and Innovation in the Massachusetts Economy." Speech given at The University of Massachusetts at Boston (September 22).

————. 1987. "The U.S. Trade Deficit and Our International Competitive Position." Lecture given in the John M. Olin Distinguished Lecture Series in International Business, Fletcher School of Law and Diplomacy, Tufts University: Medford, MA (April 9).

————. 1987. Commencement Address, Bentley College. Waltham, MA (May 16).

————. 1987. Speech to the U.S. Conference of Mayors. Nashville, TN (June 15).

———— AND ALDEN S. RAINE. 1987. *Creating the Future: Opportunity, Innovation, and Growth in the Massachusetts Economy.* Massachusetts Governor's Office of Economic Development (May).

ERIKSON, ERIK H. 1969. *Ghandi's Truth.* New York: Norton.

EWERS, H.J. AND R.W. WETTMAN. 1980. "Innovation-Oriented Regional Policy." *Regional Studies* 14:161–180.

FERGUSON, RONALD F. AND HELEN F. LADD. 1986. *Economic Performance and Economic Development Policy in Massachusetts.* Discussion Paper D86-2, JFK School of Government, Harvard University, The State, Local, and Intergovernmental Center (May).

FLYNN, PATRICIA. 1984. "Lowell: A High Technology Success Story." *New England Economic Review* (September–October): 39–49.

GABE, VERNON D. 1983. "An Outline of a Corporate Site Location Procedure." *Industrial Development* 152 (September–October): 23–25.

GALBRAITH, J.K. 1967. *The New Industrial State*. Second ed. Boston: Houghton-Mifflin.

GARDNER, W. DAVID. 1981. "Route 128: Boston's Hotbed of Technology." *Datamation* (November): 110–113.

GOLDMAN, MARSHALL I. 1984. "Building a Mecca for High Technology." *Technology Review* 87 (May–June): 6–8.

HACK, GEORGE D. 1984. "The Plant Location Decision-Making Process." *Industrial Development* 153 (September–October): 31–33.

HARDING, CHARLES F. 1982. "Company Politics in Plant Location." *Industrial Development* 151 (September–October): 19–20.

HEKMAN, JOHN S. AND JOHN S. STRONG. 1981. "The Evolution of New England Industry," *New England Economic Review* (March–April): 35–46.

HILL, CHRISTOPHER T., AND JAMES M. UTTERBACK. 1979. *Technical Innovation for a Dynamic Economy*. New York: Pergamon Press.

HILL, JOANNE AND JOEL L. NAROFF. 1984. "The Effect of Location on the Performance of High Technology Firms." *Financial Management* (Spring): 27–36.

KANTER, ROSABETH MOSS. 1983. *The Change Masters*. New York: Simon and Schuster.

———. 1977a. *Men and Women of the Corporation*. New York: Basic Books.

———. 1977b. *Work and Family in the United States: A Critical Review and Agenda for Research and Policy*. New York: Russell Sage Foundation.

———, Paul S. Myers, and Barry A. Stein. 1987. "Competitiveness Lessons from the 'Massachusetts Miracle' " *Management Review* (July): 24–26.

KENNEY, CHARLES. 1986. "The Comeback State." *The Boston Globe Magazine* (May 18): 14 + .

KIESCHNICK, MICHAEL. 1979. *Venture Capital and Urban Development*. Washington, D.C.: The Council of State Planning Agencies.

LITTLE, ROGER G. 1986. "The Photovoltaics Center: It's Good for Massachusetts." *Mass High Tech* (June 23–July 6): 12.

LLOYD, PETER E. AND PETER DICKEN. 1977. *Location in Space! A Theoretical Approach to Economic Geography.* New York: Harper and Row.

MALECKI, EDWARD J. 1981. "Science, Technology, and Regional Economic Development: Review and Prospects." *Research Policy* 10:312–334.

Massachusetts Department of Education. 1987. "Massachusetts Public School Improvement Act of 1985: A Snapshot of Program Implementation." (March).

Massachusetts *Governor's Commission on the Future of Mature Industries.* Final Report (June 1984).

Massachusetts Office of Training and Employment Policy. 1987. "Program and Financial Status Report." (May).

Massachusetts Special Commission on Tax Reform. 1986. "The Competitiveness of the Massachusetts Tax System." Final Report (October 29).

Massachusetts Taxpayers Foundation, Inc. 1986. *The Massachusetts Primer: Economics and Public Finance.* Boston: Massachusetts Taxpayers Foundation.

———. 1987. *Training People to Live Without Welfare.* Special Report. Boston: Massachusetts Taxpayers Foundation.

MILLER, ROGER AND MARCEL COTE. 1985. "Growing the Next Silicon Valley," *Harvard Business Review* 63 (July–August): 114–123.

MOHL, BRUCE. 1987. "Dukakis' Dilemma on Defense Spending." *Boston Globe* (July 26): 1+.

MOSCOVITCH, EDWARD. 1986. "The Massachusetts Miracle." *The Wall Street Journal* (July 8): 28.

NEUSTADT, RICHARD E., AND ERNEST R. MAY. 1986. *Thinking in Time: The Uses of History for Decision Makers.* New York: Free Press.

NORTH, DOUGLASS C. 1955. "Location Theory and Regional Economic Growth." *The Journal of Political Economy* 57:243–258.

Opportunity for Every American. 1986. Report of the Industrial and Entrepreneurial Economy Committee of the Democratic Policy Commission (September).

Partnership in Training: A Handbook for Program Developers. 1986. Prepared by the Bay State Skills Corporation. Boston, MA (October).

PIERCE, NEAL R. 1987. "Dukakis' Home-Grown Crop." *Boston Globe* (August 23).

———, and Carol Steinbach. 1985. "Massachusetts, After Going from Rags to Riches, Looks to Spread the Wealth." *National Journal* (May 25): 1227–1231.

"Prospectus 1986: How Long Will the Good Times Last in Massachusetts? A Special Section on the Region's Economy." 1986. *Boston Globe* (January 26).

REES, JOHN, GEOFFREY J. HEWINGS, AND HOWARD A. STAFFORD (eds.), 1981. *Industrial Location and Regional Systems.* New York: J.F. Bergin Publishers.

RESSLER, RALPH. 1983. "Manpower Training in Site Selection." *Industrial Development* 152 (March–April): 21–23.

ROGERS, EVERETT M. 1983. *Diffusion of Innovations.* Third ed. New York: The Free Press.

ROSENBERG, RONALD. 1985. "What Companies Look For." *High Technology* (January): 30–37.

RUBLIN, HEDDA L. 1986. "How Has the State of Massachusetts Percieved and Carried Out the 'Targets for Opportunity' Strategy? A Case Study of Southeastern Massachusetts," JFK School of Government, Harvard University (April), unpublished.

SABEL, CHARLES F. AND GARY B. HERRIGEL. 1987. "Losing a Market to a High-Wage Nation." *The New York Times* (June 14).

SCHECTER, DOROTHY A. 1985. "Lowell: Mill Town Renaissance." *Horizon* (June): 25–40.

SCHMENNER, ROGER W. 1979. "Look Beyond the Obvious in Plant Location." *Harvard Business Review* 57 (January–February): 126–132.

————. 1980. *Location Decision of Large, Multiplant Companies.* Cambridge, MA: Joint Center for Urban Studies of MIT and Harvard University.

————. 1982. *Making Business Location Decisions.* Englewood Cliffs, N.J.: Prentice-Hall.

SCHREIER, JAMES W., et al. 1975. *Entrepreneurship and Enterprise Development: A Worldwide Perspective.* Milwaukee: The Center for Venture Management.

SCHUMPETER, J. 1942. *Capitalism, Socialism, and Democracy.* New York: Harper and Row.

"The SEMTECH Report: Economic Modernization and Job Growth in Southeastern Massachusetts." 1985. A Report to Governor Michael S. Dukakis by the Commission on Southeastern Massachusetts Technology Development (June).

SHAPIRO, ALBERT. 1975. "Entrepreneurship and Economic Development." In Scheier, *et al, Entrepreneurship and Enterprise Development: A Worldwide Perspective.* Milwaukee: The Center for Venture Management, pp. 633–654.

————. 1972. "The Process of Technical Company Formation in a Local Area." In Cooper and Komives, *Technical Entrepreneurship: A Symposium.* Milwaukee: The Center for Venture Management, pp. 63–125.

SHAPIRO, WALTER. 1987. "The Duke of Economic Uplift." *Time* (July 27): 22–23.

SHRIBMAN, DAVID. 1987. "Governor Dukakis's Role in Economic Turnaround in Massachusetts Draws Questions in Campaign." *The Wall Street Journal* (July 21): 60.

SIMON, JANE. 1985. "Route 128: How It Developed and Why It's Not Likely to Be Duplicated." *New England Business* (July 1): 15–20.

SMITH, DAVID M. 1981. *Industrial Location: An Economic Geographical Analysis.* Second ed. New York: John Wiley and Sons.

STEIN, CHARLES. 1987. "Whose Miracle Was It?" *Boston Globe* (March 24): 25 + .

STENGEL, RICHARD. 1986. "A Tale of Two States: Massachusetts Back in the Vanguard." *Time* (May 26): 14–16.

STORPER, MICHAEL. 1981. "Toward a Structural Theory of Industrial Location." In John Rees, Geoffrey J.D. Hewings, and Howard A. Stafford (eds.), *Industrial Location and Regional Systems.* New York: J.F. Bergin Publishers, pp. 17–40.

TAYLOR, CHRISTOPHER L. 1981. *New Enterprises Descended from a Technically Based Company.* Cambridge, MA: MIT Sloan School, unpublished Master's thesis.

Technology, Innovation, and Regional Economic Development. 1984. Washington, D.C.: U.S. Congress, Office of Technology Assessment, OTA-STI-238 (July).

———. 1984. Appendix A: "High Technology Location and Regional Development: The Theoretical Base."

———. 1984. Appendix B: "Formation and Growth in High-Technology Firms: A Regional Assessment."

———. 1984. Appendix C: "Recent Evidence on High-Technology Industries' Spacial Tendencies: A Preliminary Investigation."

TEMPLER, MARK. 1984. *Entrepreneurial High-Technology Economic Development in Massachusetts.* Cambridge, MA: MIT Sloan School, unpublished Master's thesis.

"The Statehouses: Action and Innovation—A New Breed of Governors Upstages Washington." 1986. *Newsweek* (March 24): 30+.

THOMAS, MORGAN D. 1975. "Growth Pole Theory, Technological Change, and Regional Economic Growth." In *Papers of the Regional Science Association* 34:3–25.

WANG, AN, WITH EUGENE LINDEN. 1986. *Lessons.* Reading, MA: Addison-Wesley, pp. 230–231.

WARDREP, BRUCE N. 1985. "Factors Which Play Major Roles in Location Decisions." *Industrial Development* 153 (July–August): 72–76.

WEBBER, MICHAEL J. 1972. *Impact of Uncertainty on Location.* Cambridge, MA: MIT Press.

"What's Cooking in America's High-Tech Hot Sports?" 1985. *Black Enterprise* 15 (June): 256–264.

WHEAT, LEONARD F. 1973. *Regional Growth and Industrial Location.* Lexington, MA: Lexington Books.

WHEATON, WILLION C. 1979. *Interregional Movements and Regional Growth.* Washington, D.C.: The Urban Institute.

"Where to Find the Sunniest Business Climate." 1987. *Business Week* (April 13): 24.

ZARR, GERALD. 1984–85. *Economic Revitalization in Massachusetts: The Experience of Lowell and Worcester Contrasted.* Washington, D.C.: United States Department of State, Foreign Service Institute, Executive Seminar in National and International Affairs.

The authors' proceeds from the sales of this book are being donated to the Commonwealth Literacy Corps, a statewide volunteer network established by Governor Dukakis and the Massachusetts Legislature in 1987 for the purpose of bringing down the barrier of illiteracy which exists for nearly half a million citizens of Massachusetts.